FEDERAL

PRESSURE

Still On Paperwork

ISBN: 978-0-578-30177-8
Distributed by Power Of Purpose Publishing
Www.PopPublishing.com
Atlanta, Ga. 30326

Table of Contents

Acknowledgements

All praises is due to Allah! Let me begin by honoring my family that's not here with me any longer, but will never be forgotten. My brother Greg, my grandma Naya, my granddaddy Joe and my grandma Reed, as well as my dad PIG. Next, I would like to shine the light on my family that's here with me, my moms, Naomi, Emma, my wife Coretha, and my daughter Lakevia. All my Hunters' and Parkers' family. Big love to all my federal pressure brothers that I mentioned throughout the pages of this book. Assalamualaikum to my Muslim brothers that's mentioned in this book. To all my supporters that read Pressure and that's joining me to read Federal Pressure. Those that read the book, posted the book, and supported off the website, then shared the message with your friends and family. Thanks a lot for your support and I appreciate you and I would like to let you know that I'm going to continue to push these books and this message.

It is my hopes and prayers after those of you who read this book, that you will pass it on to a family member or to a friend that's incarcerated. Help me give them hope and encouragement to overcome any pressure that they may be experiencing. May it be self-afflicted or brought on by the system that is designed to destroy or to break up our family units. I also ask that you support the movement, Veli Life, bringing back the real G-code, so that we can save our kids from all this black on black senseless violence.

CHAPTER ONE

"Federal Holdover"

6/6/06. I never really been one to believe in superstition. People say 666 is the mark of the beast.

It's an evil number, something bad. Well it became true in my case. That was the day the Feds put their hold on me. After leaving the courtroom, I was an emotional wreck heading back to my cell. I couldn't get the look on my girl's face out of my mind. She looked so hurt. I still was trying to process everything. This was my first time dealing with the Feds, so I really didn't know what I was up against. When the C.O. locked my cell door, all I wanted to do was sleep. I was hoping if I go to sleep and wake up none of this would be happening to me. This had to be a bad dream. One of the nightmares that I had been having lately. My celly was this G.D. nigga named Q Tip. He was cool, but he loved to talk a lot about nothing. He had a year county time for a shootout he wasn't supposed to be in. I knew him from the town. He grabbed for me before, so when I got back to the cell he hit me with a thousand questions about what had happened in court. I knew if I didn't say something he wouldn't stop talking so I could get some sleep. I told him the Feds picked up my case. You should have seen the look he gave me. Now I knew how serious this was. Well, I could forget about going to sleep.

Q Tip started telling me stories about homies he knew that were in the Feds and been gone forever. Then, this white boy in the cell next to us joined the conversation. He let me know that I could look for nothing less than 10 years fucking with the Feds. He was speaking from experience. According to him, the Feds used this thing called a Sentencing Guideline. It was based on the charges you had and your criminal history. They also had a mandatory minimum for drug charges. The worst was for crack cocaine: 100-to-1 for crack versus powder.

They were just as tough on gun charges with enhancements for having the gun in relation to another charge. They had a name for it: *Trigger Lock.* That's when you had a gun charge and dope charge. I learned all this information about the Feds that night talking to the white boy and Q-Tip. Can't say it helped me feel better, but at least I knew what to expect now.

I was still not ready to accept going away to the Feds for all that time. The most time I had ever been locked up for was 7 years. And that felt like it would never end. So I couldn't imagine what it would feel like doing 10 years or more. I was 31 years old and had already spent all my 20s in prison. Now it was looking like I would be doing my 30s and part of my 40s in prison. I thought about all them old guys that I had left in state prison. The dudes I said I would never become. How mad they used to be with everybody and everything. Us young guys used to make fun of them using names like "Mad Dad" or "Old School." I couldn't believe this was happening to me. I went to sleep that night thinking about my future in the Feds. The next week in Knox County Jail went by fast. I got a visit from my girl that weekend. That would be my last visit by anybody for years.

The following Monday, the Federal Marshal was there to pick me up. We made the short ride from Knox County to the Federal building.

Once I got there, they processed me and two other guys into the system. I went in front of the judge the same day. I could tell right away that it was another level. My first time walking in a federal courtroom, I was in awe. I could feel the authority of the room. Everything looked fresh and new decked out in polished oak with an official American flag. It was empty except for my lawyer, prosecutor, the judge, Marshals and me. I was used to state courtrooms that were always full of people. It didn't matter if they were not there for you, it still made you feel like you weren't by yourself. In here, I felt alone. Like they could do whatever they wanted to me and get away with it. This hearing wasn't anything but an initial appearance to see if the judge granted me bail. I was denied bail. The judge considered me a flight risk because I was from out of town and my charges were drugs and guns.

The Marshals took me in the back of the holding cell. After the other two guys had been denied bail as well, we were reloaded into the back of the van and transferred to Blunt County Jail in a nearby county. Blunt County held federal inmates among state and county offenders. I had heard about Blunt County from dudes in Knox County. They called it "Bean County" because the meals always included beans and a piece of cornbread. I would find out how true this was the first week in Bean County.

I was put in 23/1 again. My new celly was from Alabama. His name was Fat Boy and it fit him. He was like 300 pounds and snored like a grizzly bear. But other than that, we got along real good. Fat Boy had been riding Bean County for 6 months. So he gave me the rundown on everything, but before he talked, he always took a handful of wet toilet paper and plastered it on the speaker box that was on the wall in all the cells. We could press a button if we needed something from the C.O. sitting in the control booth. It was a two-way speaker, so we never knew when they had it on, so we just played it like it was always on and mostly it was!

The first thing Fat Boy put me up to was the same thing my lawyer and white boy back in Knoxville jail told me: Never talk about your case with nobody in jail because you don't know who was trying to work off their time by jumping on your case. And just about everybody in Blunt County was telling on somebody. I felt like there was nobody I could trust. I could tell Fat Boy was going through the same shit. He was paranoid and making me feel the same.

There was a wild ass GD nigga in the next cell named Twin Hight. He didn't give a fuck about who knew what about his case. Every time they opened our chow flap to feed us or to give out supplies, he would get on the door talking about how his co defendant was snitching on him. His case was crazy as hell. There were two bodies involved with money, drugs, and gangbanging. Twin had his mind made up that he was going to trial.

They gave us an hour out of the cell every day. You could use this time to use the phone, to shower, or just walk around the pod. Looking around, I could tell there were five pods in a circle around the control booth. We were in Pod 2. I could look right into Pod 1 and part of Pod 3. The other pods came out for more hours a day than we did. For two months, I watched them come out for all their meals and hang out playing cards, chess, and working out. I could also tell that their pods were mixed with state and Federal inmates judging by their colored wristbands. One day I asked Fat Boy how those guys got over into the other pods while we were stuck in a lock down pod. He told me that we could go over there if we wanted to. I couldn't believe it. All this time all I had to do was a cop out (Request to Staff) to the C.O. in the control booth saying I didn't have no problem with nobody in open population and they would move me out of lock up. Fat Boy said he didn't want to be around all them rat ass niggas. I couldn't blame him, but shit, I was tired of being in the cell all day. I would just stay to myself. It had to be a few real niggas out there.

That same day, I submitted my cop out to the C.O. They moved me to open population in Pod 4. I hate that I was leaving Fat Boy like that. We got down them two months in the cell together, but I needed to be able to move around some. I had to be able to take my mind off what I was going through. My new celly was named Tony. He was a little older, and this was his second time in the Feds. Straight out the gate, I had a bad vibe about Tony. He was too happy all the time like this Fed shit was a game or something. Therefore, I didn't talk to anyone about my case, but that didn't stop him from talking about his. I just listened and let him tell me how the Feds knocked him off. The more he talked, the better my understanding of what type of nigga he was. This nigga was a cold crackhead. He might have been a real hustler back in his day. But somewhere in the game he took the wrong turn and ended up getting high. He was a real smoker, the kind that smacked their lips every time they talked. Nevertheless, we were in the same bag right now. Looking around at some of the other niggas in the pod, it seemed like the Feds were picking up any and everybody nowadays. Shit to be all the way 100%, I shouldn't be in the Feds. They didn't catch me with no brick or anything heavy at all. Word was they were picking up all the gun cases in the city. I just got fucked up at the wrong time. Back to this nigga Tony my celly. During one of his talking spells, he called himself giving me the breakdown on the Feds. He had my full attention. No matter what I thought of him he still knew more about the Feds than me. He started off by telling me there are only two types of niggas in the Feds: "The ones that told" and "The ones that wish they told." Then he paused for a moment like he was giving his words time to sink in and to see what kind of nigga I was? So I killed that right off.

I said. "Naw, there got to be some real niggas up there like me?"

The next thing this nigga said fucked me up. "Real niggas? Man, that shit went out with bell bottoms!"

I needed to hear no more. That statement was enough for me. This nigga Tony was a rat, snitch, hot nigga, whatever you wanted to call them. He justified his point of view with a story about how niggas kept it real on his first bid. He told me that when he got out, then same niggas was on, but showed him no love. So to him, that gave him a reason to snitch on anybody he wanted to. I didn't even try to explain to him how crazy that sounded. Then he changed the subject and gave me some info about the Feds that I thought was useful. The Feds pay you to work no matter what job you get. They had cable TV, microwaves, and some spots still had weights. He kept talking, but my mind was somewhere else. Now I was thinking about the last conversation I had with my lawyer. He advised me to take a plea on my case. He told me that the Feds had a 98% conviction rate. With my charges I was facing a Life sentence. They were offering me a 20-year deal, which didn't sound like a "deal" to me. At 85% of any fed sentence to be served, that was still a long time. I would be in my 50s when I got out. I had just done 11 years in the state, stayed out for four and a half years, before doing another 7 years. Now, I have only been out for 3 years and he is telling me to plea out to 20 years. God, this can't be happening to me. But, it was. I was sitting in this cell listening to this hot ass nigga talk.

There were a few real dudes in Pod 4. We ended up forming a little group. We had one rule: Paperwork. In the Feds, every defendant is provided with a Presentence Investigation ("PSI") that details everything about you and your case. We required a presentation of everybody's PSI once they were presented with it for review. There were four of us; Ron, Shawn C, Tay, and me. A few other niggas would come around, but I didn't count them because they were not in federal custody. Every time they let us out of the cells, we would meet up under the staircase and chill. Shawn C and I would work out, doing pushups and pull-ups off the stairs. Then we would do dips off the shower walls. Shawn C had been in Blunt County longer than all of us. He was playing the psychic card on them. Bro had been shot in the head before. We had the same kind of dope and gun charges. But they offered Bro 15 years, but Shawn had just got out of the state. So he wasn't trying to go right back with double digits. I felt him on that, we were in the same boat. But I can't lie, his 15 was sounding better than my 20. I was thinking like the state time, get low and go! Ron was facing 15 years on a gun case but it was a mandatory sentence because they labeled him an armed career criminal. Tay was looking at 10 years on a dope charge. He only had power cocaine so he was really good, compared to the rest of us. There were other Fed niggas in the pod.

It wasn't hard for me to tell who was hot, rat niggas because all you had to do is sit back and watch how they move. They ran around the pod playing, always laughing about anything that happened. Then they were always running up on whoever was new in the pod-like they were the Federal waiting committee asking niggas about their cases or what's up with this or that nigga? It was so bad, they weren't even trying to hide the fact that they were working for the D.A.

This one nigga named Black from Memphis was the ringleader. This nigga had been in the pod for 16 months. It was no secret he was hot. This nigga had a D.A.'s card with the number on it. I would find out later that this was the G.D. nigga snitching on Twin Hype. But on the flip side, I could also read the faces of other niggas in the pod that was real and going through the same struggle I was dealing with. How to make myself take 20 years? The Feds weren't discriminating on who they picked up. There were guys in wheelchairs, walking with canes, blind, old, young, and of all races. The Feds were a man-eating machine. This shit was bigger than little old me. Every day in Blunt County seemed like the same day. It reminded me of a movie on the Twilight Zone or the movie *Groundhog Day* when the day kept repeating itself. Then there were days when something out of the ordinary happened.

One of those days was when they brought this nigga in from Memphis for killing the weed lady out the hood in Knoxville. I had heard about the case on the radio, it was big news down in K-Town because the way they killed the old lady was uncalled for and senseless. They shot her down with a shotgun after beating her first making off with a few dollars and some $5 bags of weed. It was a shame the way they did that old lady. It could have been any of our grandmas. It was safe to say I didn't like that nigga from day one. They put him in the cell with one of my guys, Ron. I had already made up my mind the first time the dude got out of line I was going to knock him out. He was going to make it easy for me. For some reason, he felt the need to walk around mean mugging everybody. He never came over to where me and the guys hung under the stairs. He hung out with his homeboy, that rat Black from Memphis. Me and the guys would have a good laugh out of that partnership. He might not have known, but his man Black was gathering info on him for the D.A.

Ron had already told us that the nigga talked too much about his case. I never even spoke to him and I knew how the Feds picked him up, so did everybody else in the pod. It seemed the dumb ass nigga went to the pawn shop with the shotgun he used on the murder case and tried to pawn it. Who in their right mind would do something like that? Every nigga in the hood knew that pawn shops are ran by the police. But you could tell this nigga wasn't the sharpest pencil in the box. That's how the Feds got onto this sucker. But according to the word, his homie was spreading around the pod, the D.A. would be really favorable to anybody that would come forward with info that could help their case on murder against buddy. It seemed that their case was weak without any witnesses. All they had on him was the shotgun. And it was going to be hard to convince a jury that this nigga was dumb enough to commit murder and then try to pawn the murder weapon. So they sent him to Pod 4 with his homie the rat.

Boy, the Feds played a dirty game to win cases! They had a saying in Blunt County: "Why do 10 years, when you can give it to a friend?" Shit like that made me understand why Fat Boy stayed on lockdown 23/1. These pods were full of rats trying to work their time off. I got my chance to whoop grandma killer's ass. What happened was, they had been playing poker for commissary. It really was none of my business because I don't gamble. But I didn't like buddy anyway. Him and his homie the rat was trying to jump on this dude. The dude was doing county time. He wasn't Feds, but he was cool with me. He would break me off when he won big, so I felt obligated to help him out. They had him in Ron's cell cornered off when I stepped in the cell. They both turned around in surprise to see me. Somebody outside the cell pushed the door shut.

Grandma killer started to say something to me but my right hook stopped him mid-sentence. I opened up a can of Whoop Ass on him: hooks, upper cuts, the whole package. The rat and my nigga was going at it. When the smoke cleared, there was blood all over the cell. I made it out in good shape. My hands were sore after the rumble in the cell. Grandma killer and Black were quiet in the pod for a few days.

I kept my same routine working out with Shawn C and sitting under the staircase. The Feds ran a chain to Federal prison twice a week. You could leave on Monday morning or Friday, time went by pretty fast, watching niggas go and come. The pod kept flipping. The new niggas was like TV to me. I watch them come in and fall right into the rat traps. Talking about their case, and everything else that was going on in the street. Believe it or not, the Federal Marshal gets most of their intel on the hood from these hot ass niggas in jail. That's why niggas usually cut niggas off once the Feds pick them up. That's fucked up because real niggas get put in the same bag sometimes.

Like in my situation, here I was sitting in a county jail out of town, and my only family up here was my brother Hound. I called him on my nigga's three-way. He had a bunch of questions for me. What was I charged with? Did the Feds pick up my case? How much time was I facing? And the one question he wanted to know the most was were they asking about him? And what was I going to do? I assured him that I'm a G and the code was real with me. He promised to send me some money,   I never got it! And he stopped answering my calls. I got the message. I was on my own. I was used to it. This wasn't the first time I had to survive in jail.

As the weeks turned into months, my little crew was catching their time and moving on. One thing about the Feds was they pushed their caseload right on through. The average Federal case usually takes between 8-10 months to be done. Anything over that had other reasons, like somebody snitching while their co-defendant is fighting in trial. Ron decided not to play with the Feds and jumped on the 15 years they were offering him. Tay got a good deal. His plea came down to 8 years. When he came back from court and told us that I was very curious to see his paperwork. Ron had already shown the crew his work. Everything was good with him: No 5K1 downward departure in his case. The nigga Tay never produced his paperwork. Ron left a week later and Tay left the following week. I was next up.

It was the one of the hardest things I ever did in my life. But I prayed to Allah, him not to let me do all this time. I kept my self-respect, my honor, and stood ten toes down. I played that game how it was supposed to go, by the G-Code. But most importantly, I held fast to my faith in Islam, that Allah would answer my prayer. I copped out to 20 years, but when my PSI came back I fell in the sentence guideline of 262-327 months. The Judge gave me the low end, 262 months. That's 21 years, 10 months. Standing in that courtroom by myself, it felt like I was being buried alive. It used to be a time when a 25-year sentence was considered as Life. And here I was with 22 years. When the Judge slammed that gavel and sentenced me, I will never forget what he said.

"Mr. Hunter, the court has determined you to be a Career Criminal. I see by your record you served two sentences in the state of Florida."

I said, "Yes."

He went on to tell me that I should have an easy time adjusting to Federal prison. It's a lot easier than doing state time in Florida.

I didn't know if his words were meant to make me feel better. It wasn't working. All I could think of was how my mom was going to take this news. And how old my daughter would be once I got out. Those were the thoughts that were running through my mind as the judge was handing down my Federal sentence. My eyes were open and I was standing on my feet. But it was like a dream. The judge was asking me things and I guess I was answering him because he kept talking. Then I felt the Marshall's hands on me leading me out the courtroom. I was put in the holding cell. About two hours later, me and the other four guys were loaded up in the transfer van, heading back to Blunt County. I went back to my cell and fell straight to sleep.

Later on, when we came out to eat dinner, me and Shawn C did our workout. After that, we showered up. I told him what happened in court. How much time I took. I could tell he was thinking about his situation. Once I took the time and the damage was done something inside you clicked. My mind went into survival mode. I was ready to get on the next step of the Federal journey. I hate I was leaving Shawn C by himself, over the months we had become cool, supporting each other throughout this struggle while we both were in the Feds. That night when they locked us down, I cried to Allah in prayer. I needed help making sense of my life. This bid would put me over the halfway mark of being locked up more than I had been free in my life. I knew I broke laws and doing time was part of that. But it seemed like I never caught a break. It has always been prison for me.

I have never been the one to make a big deal of feeling sorry for myself. What good would that do for me? Nothing is going to change my life, but me. As my celly was asleep, I laid awake reflecting over my life and being honest with myself. I was looking at things truthfully. I was able to see that Allah was saving me, not punishing me with this time. I looked at all the times I could have died out there, but he saved me. I thought about all my homies that were dead and the ones with life sentences that would never be released. All the ones I left in prison that I hadn't done more for. The more truthful I was, the more blessed I felt. That's when my prayers changed from regret and sorrow to thanking Him, and seeking help on becoming a better man. That night in my cell I had a spiritual encounter with God.

It was like he wanted me to depend on Him. I didn't have anybody with me. I was alone in court. Alone in jail. Now, I was headed to

Federal prison (anywhere in the country). I had to put my trust in God. All I asked Him for was to help me change my life and not let me do all this time. Twenty years was too long. I promised Him that I was going to try hard with my dean; Islam. And I wasn't smoking or drinking anymore. That was it. No more drugs, not even selling them. I don't know what time I finally went to sleep, but I slept for almost two days. I missed all the meals that next day and I didn't care.

I remember Shawn C coming by to check on me. The day after I came back, I was ready to bid. Workout was in full effect. I kept trying

to talk Shawn C into taking the 15 years. Things had got a little tougher for Shawn C instead of coming down with their plea offer. The government superseded his indictment with new charges. I felt bad for my dog, and I knew how much pressure he was under. This was another level. This was the Federal Government vs. Young Black Men. I gave him the best advice I could.

"Turn to Allah, bro. Keep your faith in Him. Don't fold like the rest of these suckers are doing all around us. Everything happens for a reason, we got to use this time to figure out what God is trying to show us."

Shawn C just nodded his head like he was feeling me, but his eyes said a different story. I didn't know what else to say, so I fell silent. It was time for lockdown. We gave each other dap and headed back to our cells. The next couple of days passed by like normal. Blunt County was back to being the Twilight Zone. Same old thing every day like clockwork. Lock in, lock out, get fed, guys come in, guys left. Then it was my time to catch the federal prison run.

I was awakened early this morning. The C.O. told me to roll it up. Meaning my mat and bed roll. I stopped by Shawn's cell and said my goodbyes. And then I joined the line of other dudes leaving for prison and court that day. It was October 10, 2007 (9 days after my daughter's birthday). That's why I remember the day so well. Because I kept reminding myself to send her a card when I got the chance.

Walking into Federal prison was totally different from state prison for me. I was used to having homies waiting on me being received with big respect because of my reputation from the streets and jail. I always got respect when I came to state prison. But here in the Feds, the first thing that matters was who you were with. Dudes were grouped into groups that are called "cars." A car is made up by where a person was from, or what set (gang) he was affiliated with. Cars were made up by race, and even religion. Once you were with your car, then the big question was: Are you hot (a rat, snitch, informant, government witness). The car needed to see your paperwork (court documents). They needed to know that there were no rats riding in their car before they pledged their lives and loyalty to them, before you were able to walk the yard. That was one of the ways the Feds was different from the state. In the state there was always somebody there that was in the county jail, or from your hood that knew if you were solid and not a rat. But in the Feds, you could be sent somewhere with none of your homeboys.

Like my situation I was in while in Kentucky, there wasn't a real Florida car there. They had a small South car. I would find out later there was only one more nigga there from Miami. He had life, and been gone 19 years already. He was an older homie and he wasn't on anything at all. He stayed out the way, working in Unicor. When I walked on the cell block the C.O. told me to find a cell on my own. So I asked the first nigga I saw about an empty bunk. He answered my question with a question asking me where I was from? It was a reasonable question. So I told him I was from Miami.

"Oh, you from Florida!"

I wanted to correct him but he was right in a way. It's a Florida thing that us Miami niggas like to think of Miami being an island of its own.

No disrespect to the rest of Florida, that was just our arrogant mind set. The dude yelled upstairs to some dude they were calling J-Ville. I guess that was short for Jacksonville, Florida. This young light skin nigga came running downstairs. He looked mixed. But, yeah, like I thought he was from Florida. He said what's up, and the dude told him I was his homie from Miami. J-Ville looked like he was happy to see me. I would find out real soon, that it wasn't a lot of Florida niggas up here. J-Ville took over and we went looking for a cell for me. When I asked him was there any Muslims on the block he smiled and said, "Hell yeah, you Muslim?"

"Yeah."

Then he said, "That's going to make it easier because the Muslims keep beds open for their brothers." That's when he took me to meet Amin Saad from Jersey.

Everybody called him Saad. He and J-Ville were cool. I gave him the salam and he greeted me as well. And from that moment, Allah blessed me with a real brother for life. Saad took me to his cell, gave me a laundry bag of all new supplies. They called this a "care package." Then he asked me what size shoes I wore. All I could say was it was meant to be because we both were the same size and he gave me a pair of white Air Force 1s. We left his cell. He took me to meet the rest of the brothers on the block. J-Ville was right, the Muslims were strong on this block. I would later find out that it was the block with the most Muslims on the whole compound. The Imam was this big brother from overseas named Salamoon. He had a set of big beads. He was the one that found me a cell. It was with this D.C. dude that wasn't Muslim but most of his homies were. He was older than me and we had another celly that was leaving in a week. I would get his bottom bed when he left. He was a cool dude from Georgia. I set my paperwork on the desk and told both of them they could read it whenever they felt like it. I had already shown Saad and J-Ville so the word was spreading through the block that I was on real nigga time, but I was Muslim.

Being in the Feds was going to be an adjustment for me. I was used to doing state time and being the shot caller for my city. The Feds were broken down by states and gangs. I had a lot to learn when it came to gang culture. The prison I was at in Manchester, Kentucky. The biggest cars were Tennessee, Kentucky, and Ohio. There was a coalition among the Crips, GDs, Bloods, Latin Kings, and Vice Lords so they could match numbers with the Mexican gangs (The Mexican Mafia, Surenos, MS 13 and Paisa). I had to get an understanding of Federal prison politics. My approach to doing time was I wanted to change my life. I was focused on my promise to God. So I got with the brothers that were

on their dean in the religion.

I got a job in Food Service. I knew I would be able to get a hustle on in there. But I also had my name on the waiting list to work in the Unicor factory. It was the highest paying job on the compound. Niggas were making between $300 to $1,000 a month. One thing I could say about Federal prison was there was money on the yard. I didn't have to sell dope or rob nobody to eat. That made it easier for me to stay out of trouble. I did just that. I went to work. I would work out in the afternoon, then I hung out in the dorm on the block with the old heads watching the news. I played a few games of chess, prayed with the brothers, then locked down, read and slept. All that would be repeated the next day. Doing time is all about getting a set routine going and sticking to it.

I was building bonds with real niggas from all over, even amongst the brothers in the kitchen at work like big bro Mel aka Jahmel. He was from Ohio. Big Ahk aka Yakubi was from New York. I got real cool with Leon from Nashville, Tennessee. We started working in the kitchen at the same time. Then there was Red Dog from Memphis, Tennessee. He was one of the cooks. Muscle Head was a Crip from L.A. and my dog

Ron from Blunt County was working there as well. Me and Leon used to steal anything we could get our hands on. From bananas to bread, somebody always wanted something from the kitchen. I was doing alright, not needing to call out to the world for nothing, but to see how my family was doing.

I got heavy in the law studying my case. I would spend hours in the law library looking for loopholes in my case. I got good at understanding case law. Guys started coming to see me asking questions about their case. It got so bad that dudes would bring me their homie's paperwork to look over to see if they cooperated with the government. They wanted to know were they a snitch or not. So my stamp became official on the yard. If I gave the all-clear you were good to walk the yard. Don't get me wrong, I wasn't the only one with an official stamp. And everybody's car wasn't all the way real. You had some cars on the yard that was cuffing hot niggas aka Rats. Then on the other hand, niggas was getting checked in off every bus that came in. Some went willingly, others got that banger put on them.

I moved in a cell with a Muslim. He was an older brother from Tennessee. His name was Leonard, but we called him Lenny. His Muslim name is Jamal. Bro ran a store, so our cell stayed busy. Saad had a store too, but he wasn't trying to make any money off it. I think Saad just likes keeping his locker stocked with everything. And because everybody knew he had everything they used to come ask him all the time. So he just made a store to cut down on all the beggars. Saad was always looking out for the brothers. The Imam stayed in Saad's locker. Salamoon loved to cook. He was actually good at it, so Saad ended up financing a cheesecake business for Salamoon. It started going good. On Friday after Jumah service, a lot of brothers would put in orders for the cakes and Salamoon would sell out. He had orders on the block. But we didn't know until later that for every cake bro made, he would make one for himself. He didn't eat the whole cake. He would often come around to all the brothers and give us slices. We took care of each other in my unit. The Muslims had respect from all the cars on the yard.

We had brothers from D.C. that were Muslim. Some of them still concerned themselves with the D.C. car. I got along with all them D.C. dudes, Muslims and non-Muslim. In the Feds, D.C. guys had a bad label on them. A lot of it had to do with the fact that the Feds was their state joint. Meaning no matter what you did in D.C. you broke the law, you were going to the Feds. So they had homies that was just wild ass street niggas, some who were locked up for petty crimes. Me being used to doing state time, and being locked up with all kinds of niggas I understood the mindset of a wolf. It preys on the weak. I used to be wild just like them. So there was no pressure on me, but for weak niggas it was pressure being around most D.C. niggas. And another thing I like about the D.C. boys was they were big on paperwork. They kept their car clean, so niggas could say this or that about them. Every yard I been on with them, they were hard on hot niggas and were all ready to ride on some race shit when it came down to the Mexicans or white boys. And because I wasn't hot, and I was Muslim, all the D.C. dudes gave me respect. I got love from Chicago (the "Land") guys too. My Chicago dog was "Westside" aka Vince; he was a Black Crow.

Whatever car you were in, you was responsible for making sure you was solid then you got stamped as a real nigga. For example, if a nigga came on our block from Florida, it was up to me to check his work. Once I did that, I could stamp him. Then niggas would give him his *Real Nigga Rights*. The only way some other niggas from another car would feel like they had a right to see your paperwork was if you was moving into their cell. So if a nigga from another car, city, or state see a nigga walking the yard with me or eating, talking or taking group pictures with me they would automatically assume that nigga was a real niggs. And it was the same with me. If I seen a new nigga sitting at the gang's table, or walking the yard with one of them I would assume that nigga was on count: A real nigga.

Because I got knocked off in Tennessee, I had a Tennessee number (-074). That was one of the ways you could figure out where dudes were from in most cases. But there were those cases like mine, where I'm from Miami, but I got jammed up in Tennessee. I was cool with a lot of niggas from Knoxville, or they knew my brother. I got real tight with a lot of niggas out of Nashville, most were Crips, a few Bloods, a couple were G.D's. My young nigga Celo was a real nigga and was Bout It, Bout It! He had the Crip car, let him tell it. I could never tell who was calling the shots for them. There were so many on the yard from all over. For a while I thought it was the big dog from L.A. Muscle Head. It didn't matter if something popped off you would see all them niggas on the yard together ready to ride. The Crip car was made up with niggas from all over. We even had Muslim brothers that was still Crip. The Imam used to be on all the brothers that were on gang time. He had to be because what if a situation arose and the Muslim got into it with one of the gangs? We had to know where they stood. I was kind of glad that I was so far away from all my homies.

It was only one dude from Miami up there at first, and he was older and out the way. But as time passed, a few more would come from Florida, but not Miami for the most part. They were laid back like J-Ville and Tee from Tallahassee. They both knew I was on Muslim time, but at the same time I had their back. But I also let them know that if something jumped off with them, don't wait on the politics. Take off and go hard on your man because we don't have no numbers and theses niggas or whoever ain't shooting no head up fade. I had some more Crips I was cool with like Dee Da Deuce and CeeLo. They were 52 Crips from Nashville and lived on the same block with me. Since I told y'all about paperwork and the Crips, it's only right that I mention this story ...

Well, I already told you I was one of the go-to men with the law and stamping niggas on their work. Normally a dude's homeboy would bring his homie's work to me to see what was up with them. But this time was different. We had this young nigga from Alabama come in the unit. He was a Crip. So CeeLo let him move in the cell with him. He knew that CeeLo was big on seeing that paperwork asap. So when it came instead of giving it to CeeLo, he brought it to me knowing if I stamped it he was good. When it came to stamping a nigga's paperwork, I took it real serious. I wasn't going to label you a rat or stamp you solid unless I was certain. It was a time when I would go get a second opinion. In this nigga Bam's situation I didn't have to, I found red flags all through his Docket Sheet. It said that after he was arrested by the Feds, he went to be released into the Marshal's custody for 40 days. That was a major red flag. And after 40 days, he came back to court then they gave him a bond. That was two red flags. So when CeeLo came to ask me what's the word on Bama, I showed him what I found and then gave him my opinion. I couldn't stamp Bama.

We called Bama up to my cell. I asked him to explain the 40-day thing and why would the prosecutor put in a motion to get him released? At first he tried to act like he didn't know what I was talking about. He thought just because his paperwork didn't say 5K1 downward departure that I would miss the other red flags. I had a trained eye for red flags. Like when your indictment had a lot of seals on it. Sometimes that meant something was up in your case. CeeLo and the rest of the Crip homies put pressure on Bama. He came clean and told the truth. When he was free for 40 days he was working for the Feds. I never found out exactly what he did, maybe buys, setting niggas up. Nevertheless, they put hands on him and sent him up to check into protective custody ("PC").

Your reputation and word is everything to men in prison. Nobody wanted a rat in their car. I wasn't taking no chance on me stamping a nigga then it coming out later that he was hot. So even though Bama wasn't in my car, if I would have told CeeLo he was good, I would've looked like I was cuffing a hot nigga. So I wasn't mad that they sent him up. He should've never put me in the middle of that. It was always some mess going on about paperwork. A little bit after Bama got ran up, two niggas came on the unit from Florida. They came about a week apart, I couldn't believe it. Didn't too many dudes from Florida come up on the mountain top, yeah Manchester sat on top of a mountain. But every so often, one would get off the bus. I always checked to see if they had a -004 or -018 number. Those were South Florida numbers. So to get two in one month was out of the ordinary. Also, both coming to the same dorm was strange to me. Because they were from Florida, they were brought to me.

The first one was from Miami. He was Haitian so you know we called him Zoe. I didn't know him. He was younger than me. But I knew a lot of his O.G. homies out of Little Haiti. Sticking to the code, I asked Zoe for his paperwork so I could stamp him. He told me his case was still open. He had more charges pending. That was a new one on me. I didn't know if the Feds did it like that. I thought they made you resolve all your charges before they sent you to prison. But he explained that they were state charges that the Feds were looking into. I took Zoe on his word that he wasn't hot. But I also let him know that I wasn't stamping him. And I would let the other real niggas in the unit know his situation. I still dropped a care package on him. I had a feeling Zoe was telling the truth. For now, he had a question mark on his name. One thing I learned about the Feds is that it's not as big as it seems. Word travels fast. You could run but you couldn't hide long. So if you were a rat, somebody would get off that bus and expose you.

The very next bus that came, here come the second Florida nigga. He was from CoCo Beach. Just like Zoe, he was younger t and I didn't know him. I knew a few of his O.G. homeboys from state school. The nigga CoCo was big, about 6'1", 260 pounds. My locker was hurting now, so I came off another care package for him. Then I hit him with the paperwork talk. He assured me that he knew how the game went and as soon as he got his property he would bring them to me. I was cool with that. There wasn't any pressure on me. It wasn't like I was running the Florida car because for real, there really wasn't one. The little bit of Florida niggas that were on the mountain really just stayed out the way. A couple of them were on gang time. I was just doing my part for the *Real Nigga* click of dudes that were on the same block with me. CoCo was put in the same cell as Zoe. At first things seemed like it was cool with them. CoCo came with some weed from his last spot. He was at Big Sandy U.S.P., one of the hardest penitentiaries in the BOP. That was one of the reasons I thought CoCo was a real nigga because they were killing rats up in Big Sandy. So if he made it up there, I felt like he was good. I would find later, he stayed in the whole while he was up there. They ran him in on check in ("PC"). Not to get too far ahead of the story ... back to him and Zoe. In the unit, I always sat in my doorway, when I wasn't reading or writing. From my cell doorway on the top tier, I could see everybody and everything. I also had a good view of all the TVs. But for the most part watching all the different characters that made up the unit was oftentimes more entertaining to me than what was on TV.

Zoe was laid back. He would sit by himself and watch time. He was respectful to everybody. I felt good about Zoe as a homeboy. I told myself if he needed me, I would aid and assist him. But watching CoCo move, I felt different about him. He came in the unit doing too much with his weed, running around smoking with whoever. I didn't care nothing about the weed because I didn't drink or smoke any more. But it was something about how carefree he was moving that didn't sit well with me. He was being too friendly without checking with me, his homie to find out who was who? Though my suspicion of him started to come clear.

One day after I came in from working out, Zoe was standing by my cell waiting on me. He wanted to talk to me alone. When we went into my cell, he got right to the point. He felt like CoCo was going through his paperwork. He said the nigga CoCo would have the private sign up for long period of times like he was in there using the bathroom, but he was really going through Zoe's locker. I asked Zoe if anything was missing? He said it wasn't. Then I wanted to know did he talk to CoCo about it? He hadn't. Ultimately, I wanted to know what he wanted me to do? He said he was just telling me about it to see if I could holla at somebody to let him change cells. I told him I would see what I could do for him. But in the meantime, he needed to lock his locker. Zoe took my advice, but I could tell it was tension between him and CoCo. It took me a few days but I got somebody to let Zoe move in with them. That part was settled. When Zoe moved out, CoCo caught an attitude with the both of us. I couldn't care at all. We weren't ever cool anyway. He never brought me his paperwork to look at, so that was a red flag in my book.

He started hanging close to one of my Muslim brothers named Polo from Chicago. Polo was a new Muslim and very impressionable. Polo used to shake a little weed from visit, so I thought that's why they were cool. But like I said before, in the Feds everything comes to the light. A bus came in with some new dudes from Big Sandy. One of them spotted CoCo and spread the word that he got run up at Big Sandy and that he was hot. He really started acting funny after that. Walking around the unit like somebody did something to him. About a week later, the counselor called Zoe into his office for a lawyer call. Zoe came out and told me the Feds picked up his state charges.

Come to find out it was two bodies. He was on his way back to court in the building in Miami. We didn't know then, but after Zoe went back to court, a week later, Tee, the homie from Tallahassee, got an email from Zoe's sister telling him that Zoe said his lawyer gave him a few names of some niggas that jumped on his case. Tee printed off the email, and come to find out CoCo, Polo, and another nigga from Georgia that stayed in the unit across from our unit were in the email. Because Polo was from Chicago and on count with the Vice Lords, the V.L. the shot caller put pressure on Polo so he came clean. It was all CoCo's plan: He was selling spots on Zoe's case. Yeah, you heard me right, selling downward departures on Zoe's case. Shit like that only happens in the Feds.

According to Polo, the dude from GA paid $500 to get on the case. Polo said that CoCo kept trying to convince him to jump on Zoe's case but he refused. So when all this came out, me and Tee stepped to the nigga CoCo to see what he had to say. We showed him the email from Zoe's sister. He denied it just like I told Tee he would. So we had no choice but to bring up what Polo was telling his people. CoCo said that was a lie, but here goes the twist. He claimed that Polo was the one who was trying to get him to jump on Zoe's case. Both of them were Zoe's celly in the three-man cell. So I didn't know who to believe because he could have told us that from the jump, as soon as we showed him the email.

So I told him straight up, "Bro, I don't know who is lying but somebody going up top if we find out this shit real!"

He tried to act hard talking about he wasn't hot and he was taking a nigga with him if he go up. I wasn't about to go back and forth with him. I was never one to argue with nobody. Me and Teen was bangered up just in case this nigga jump out there. And Tee could see I was about to push off, so that's when he spoke up and said that Zoe's sister said she was going to mail him the paperwork from Zoe's lawyer. So, we would know then who was on the case for real. Tee gave me the head nod like "let's Chill and wait." Me and CoCo locked eyes and I could tell by his body language he was worried.

On the very next 10-minute move, I was sitting in my doorway still thinking about this hot ass mess these niggas got me in. Ten minutes was the time they gave us to go wherever we needed to, like the rec yard or the library. Most of the time, dudes would just go out the unit to meet a homie on the walkway, to pass or get something. CoCo shot out the unit like he was going to the yard. But he really was on a check-in mission. He had a lock tied onto a belt in his hand. He ran into Polo on his way back to the unit on the walk. He chased Polo around the compound swinging that lock. They both ended up checking in on that move. When the news got back to me, I wasn't mad. I felt like that was a blessing because when that paperwork got back to us, and CoCo and the GA nigga was on the work I would have to put that banger on CoCo and check him in.

After the paperwork got around the GA nigga went ahead and checked in before he got sent up. I got so many stories where niggas are doing any and everything to get their sentences cut. I guess my old Blunt County celly was right when he said the Feds were made up of dudes who told and dudes who wished they told. I was starting to see the moves of those who wished they had told. They were filing Rule 35(b) motions.That's the name of the motion where prosecutors used cooperating inmates after they had been sentenced and gave them time cuts for snitching. But I was also right there with real niggas like myself in the Feds too. The next couple of buses that came up on the mountain dropped some real niggas in my unit. One of them was my Muslim brother from Flint, Michigan. His name was Buda. He was a young brother in his early 20's. We hit it off right away. Buda got on real nigga time with me and was still on his deen. All he wanted to do was crack jokes and eat. Yeah, Buda reminded you of a short Biggie Smalls with a Midwestern swag. Me and Buda would team up joking on old man Mr. Jackson from South Carolina. Man, talking about somebody that would have you laughing. Mr. Jackson was in on a gun charge with a 10-year Fed bid. He was a prime example of the fact that the Feds were picking up anybody. Mr. Jackson reminded you of a character off Sanford and Son. Even though he looked and acted like an ex-wino. He was a real nigga. I saw his paperwork. And for that reason alone, we accepted him as one of the guys.

A few more real guys came on the unit. There was my Muslim brothers Isha ("Love") and Amin ("Stacy") from D.C. They both became Imams over the community. Can't leave out my barber, cat from

Louisville, KY. I had some real niggas out of Ohio that were on the unit, Jazz and Chop. We were all on paperwork time, that's what made up the real niggas on the block. To me building these bonds with real niggas from different cities was a major move for the long run. I was thinking about L.A.P. ("Life After Prison.") Those connections were going to give me a hood pass in cities all over the country. I had plans to be a global dude once I was out. So it was smarter to be on Real Nigga time than just fuck with niggas from my state only. I knew niggas that did their time like that. D.C. guys were big on that. To them everybody that wasn't from D.C. wasn't on their level; they called outsiders "Bamas." It kind of reminded me of how us Miami niggas acted in out of state prisons. We call everybody that wasn't from Miami "O.B." aka Off Brands. But even back in my state prison days, I knew it was smarter to fuck with real niggas from all over Florida. So I stuck with the same mindset when it came to who I kicked it with in the Feds. I was all about supporting the real. I still walked the yard on my own. I wasn't big on moving in a pack. I didn't take group pics or hang out on the yard with dudes. Even niggas that was on Real Nigga time. Because your paperwork might be good, you could be one of the "I wish I told" niggas.

CHAPTER TWO

"Unicor: The Sweat Factory"

After going hard hustling in the kitchen stealing everything that wasn't nailed down, my request to work in the sweat factory came through. It was about time. I was ready to get some of that easy money. Listening to the other guys that were already working down there, all the jobs were easy. It was a sewing factory. They made pants for the Army. I saw a few of my Muslim brothers' paychecks. Dudes were making from $300 to $1,200 a month. That's with doing all the overtime, which I had no problem doing. I would watch them guys go to work from 7:30 AM to 8 PM. There were even times when they stayed out after the 10 PM count at work. It was almost like they lived down there in that factory. Dudes would joke about moving their bunks into the Unicor factory. There were 600 jobs in the factory. That was a third of the compound. The money was so good, dudes would hire other inmates to clean their cells, wash their clothes, even cook for them. There was a dude that was paying women to come see him. I used to laugh at them guys trying to play baller on a Fed factory job.

You had guys that had been in the factory for 10 years and more, saving money and being super tight. I didn't laugh at them because that was my plan. To work and save as much as I could. I'm not going to even front. I needed the job. And it came at the right time because things were getting tough in the Food Service. Niggas was snitching. Staff was locking the prison down for everything. We were fighting almost everyday in there. I wasn't the only one that got hired by Unicor.

My dog Ron from Blunt County and Leon from Nashville came from Food Service to the factory with me. Walking into Unicor that Monday morning, I would never forget the slave feeling that came over me. Picture a big warehouse with sewing machines from one end to the other. There were inmates at each station working. White, black,

Spanish, every race was in the factory. White skinheads, gangbangers, dope dealers, killers, straight up street niggas was all in there sewing like old women. I could remember thinking to myself, we all thought we were gangster but the Feds showed all of us who was the real gangster! I didn't know a thing about sewing machines.

I was kind of intimidated by sewing. But I always had a mindset that if somebody else can do it, so can I. They put me, Leon, and Ron in the same section. The factory was broken down into four sections. The work would start in Section 1 and end in Section 4. It came in bundles. A bundle was made up of 20 pants once it was fully done. But in the beginning a bundle could be 50 pieces of pant parts, some 25. The number varied. Being at the end of the bundle line, all of our bundles were 20. I started out on one of the easier jobs. I ran a trimmer. It looked just like a pair of hair clippers hooked up to a vacuum cleaner. My job was to trim off the loose threads left by the sewers. I made 15 cents per bundle. I would have to trim 6 bundles just to make 90 cents. I could do like 3-4 bundles in 15 minutes. So I set a goal to at least make $3.00 a day. The hardest part about the job was standing up on my feet for hours at a time. But it was the 3 of us doing it. So we would talk shit and kick it as we worked and time flew.

Going to work everyday in the factory gave me purpose. It made me feel like I was doing something positive with myself. I wanted to change. I knew I had to change my life if I ever wanted to have a normal life once I got out. To me working in Unicor meant something bigger than a prison check. Yeah, I really needed the money. Me and a lot of other guys too. But not everybody was down there in the factory just for money. After I learned how to sew real good, I could do my job without really even thinking about it. I would work and sit back listening to guys tell their story. That's how we worked and got through the day. Sharing stories some days, other days how much money we were getting and what we did with it. We talked about family and places we'd been to. There would be days of nonstop sports, yeah gambling was big talk and action in the factory. But for whatever reason we were there, all in it together. One thing we all had to overcome was our pride. Because like it or not, we were working for peanuts compared to the money we were used to getting selling drugs or robbing. Just doing whatever crime you were doing in the world. Just looking at myself, a low level street hustler, I was making two to three stacks a day dealing dope. Now I was making $7-$8 a day sewing pants.

There were big time guys working in Unicor too. I'm talking about guys dealing heavy weight in the dope game. Then you had your scammer who was ripping people off for millions. So for us to come work for little to nothing, we had to lower our pride. Even though we were locked up in prison, we were still proud men and our reputation still mattered to us. There were guys that refused to work in Unicor because they felt that it was beneath them. I would watch some of those same guys sit on the unit all day with an orderly job cleaning the bathroom or the C.O. 's office making $18-$50 a month, begging for coffee, asking for soup to eat. But because they felt like working in Unicor was a slave job, they refused it. To them, doing all the cleaning and begging was more real and cool. I could never understand their logic. Don't get me wrong, I'm very conscious. I know we were being exploited by the federal government taking advantage of us as cheap labor.

One thing I did while doing time was read. And I had the pleasure of reading *The New Jim Crow.* It explained the whole "War on drugs" plot for cheap labor. Reading that book also made me understand that this was bigger than me. Reading, studying, and practicing my religion gave me strength to endure the oppressive, unjust reality of being locked up in federal prison. Left me with no choice but to work for crumbs in the sweat factory. It was either that or stealing out the kitchen, fighting for crumbs in there, or trying to act cool working for crumbs on the unit. There were guys who didn't have to work anywhere. They still had money on the streets. The Feds didn't take everything from them. Or they had real support from the outside. For whatever reason, they could do their time however they liked.

My Muslim brother Saad was one of them. He mostly worked out, and helped run the Muslim community. He became the Imam before he ended up going to the hole for kicking a dude to sleep. On my unit, just about everybody had a job in the factory. It was just a few dudes like Saad that didn't work in Unicor. Being that Saad didn't have to work, he would spend his day studying Islamic religion books and also studying to be a personal trainer. The one thing about Saad was that he was real to the core. If he fucked with you, he was riding with you all the way, no matter what the consequences were. A situation came one morning before we were called to work.

It was still dark outside, and the breakfast meal was still being served. I will never forget coming out my cell seeing a nigga running back into the unit covered in blood screaming for help. In come Saad and his dog Philly right on buddy's heels. He fell and stumbled into a cell right below mine. Saad and Philly went up in that cell and damn near killed that boy. If it wasn't for my old celly Lenny and a few more dudes, they would have. There wasn't any need for me to go down there because he was done with. Come to find out later it was all over that nigga fucking a punk in the Philly cell. Yeah, him and Philly were cellies. Saad was just helping his dog punish this fool. Saad ended up doing 10 months in the hole behind that. They shipped Philly. He used a razor on buddy's face. That's why there was so much blood. I corrected my new job in Unicor for not being involved in that situation because I used to walk to breakfast with Saad in the morning. Since I got my new job I could afford to buy sandwiches from the guys who worked in the kitchen. So, I stopped going to breakfast. My plan was to stay out of trouble, work on my case, and save money from working in Unicor.

Before I got the job, I was getting into hustling on the side. Not drugs or gambling. There are other things to hustle like pictures of naked girls and magazines. Word was getting back to the Imam Salmoon. So one day, he and a brother from Philly named Sharod pulled up on me asking me about pictures. I told them it was true. They went into a long talk about how un-Islamic it was and how it looked bad on the community. I knew I was wrong, so I didn't even try to argue with them. I told them they were right. All they asked me to do was stop selling the pics and magazines and come to all the Islamic classes. At first I didn't know how to feel about the brothers stepping to me about what I considered to be my personal business. I was so used to being the shot caller on almost every yard I had been on.

It was different in the Feds. But I was trying to change. I promised God I would take my religion seriously for now on, brother meant well. They were teaching me my religion. So I started attending class more, and hung around the brothers. When I wasn't doing that, I was working out on the yard. But most of the time I was in the factory. Unicor was where everybody kicked it and got money. It was something new for me. It felt like a real job. I went and learned every job in my section aggressively. I wasn't by myself. Leon and Ron did too. This is how things worked in Section 4. There were the 15 cents a bundle job, all the way up to $1.80 a bundle job. The price range varied by operation. The bundle came with a ticket. You sign your name on it and take a copy for your pay sheet. That's the way they kept up on who worked on each bundle.

The ticket system was designed to keep track with how many bundles you did, and who did it. So if you messed up on the work it would come back to you to fix it. Doing rework wasn't ever a good thing, because now you was wasting time on it. You were also not making money on new work. Everyday somebody was being stuck with doing rework from the day before. We would all laugh because we knew the person was mad that they weren't making any money until it was fixed. But it wasn't funny when it was your turn. Everybody had their turn, even me. But I learned how to beat the system on rework. I would do both, a new bundle and my rework. That way it wasn't a total loss of my day. I wouldn't make the same money, like a non-rework day, but I would make some. I soon got so good that I never had to rework.

I had always been a fast learner, and when you added money to it I'm even faster. In my section there were 11 stations. I made it a goal to learn all 11 operations. I went from making $3.00 a day to $250 on most days. Some days I would make more with overtime; other times I made less. But I would go hard every time I went into the factory. Finally, me and Leon got assigned to a $100 a bundle. It was three of us assigned to the operation. The other guy was named Naz (like the rapper). He was from Virginia. We all got along. But because me and Leon was on real nigga time, We pressured Naz into bringing his paperwork in for me to look over. I found out that Naz had gotten immunity from the prosecutor in his case. After that, he no longer wanted to work with us. I guess it was uncomfortable for him being around some real niggas, that's how pressure worked. The Mexicans had the Q.A. "Quality Assessment" jobs. They were like inmate police for the factory when it came to checking our work. It was their job to look for mistakes in the bundle. They got paid straight pay while we chased ticket pay. Their money was guaranteed, by the hour. So it was chemistry for a bomb against race. I used to wonder sometimes was this some kind of Willie Lynch slave strategy. It was always some kind of tension between the black and the Mexicans because we would see them showing favoritism for their homeboys. But when it comes to our work, they go by the book and nick-pick everything. I got into it with them a lot because I knew I did good passable work. I wasn't about to let them fuck with my money.

I used to bump heads with the head shot caller for the Sureno Mexican gang out of L.A. Looking at him, you wouldn't think he was even in a gang. But it's true that looks can be deceiving. He was in his early 30s. But the word on the pound was, he was a cold-blooded killer. He had a life sentence, and he was also the head of Q.A., so he was used to being with most of the bullshit. I wanted to beat his ass more than once., and he knew it. He didn't like me and the feeling was mutual. Our day was coming, I knew it. The only reason I didn't do him sooner was because I thought about how it would blow up the yard in a race riot. If I knew it was just about us two, I would've stuck that banger in him. Even though I knew I could beat him, I knew he wasn't going to fight. It would be banger against banger.

It was a known fact on the compound that the Mexicans would not fight head up. So if it was a Black-on-Mexican beef, it would become a race matter. So I did my best to hold myself back for the greater cause. That wasn't always the case, in Unicor, it wasn't nothing to walk into the bathroom and somebody was fighting. Working in Unicor made time fly. Before you knew it, a year was gone and my savings was growing. I put myself on a real budget. I went to lunch and dinner every day, even when they had pork. I would go get the alternative, peanut butter, just to save money. I was making $500-$800 a month. I would live off $100 a month and save the rest. That went on for about 5 years for 2008-2013, then things slowed down. It would pick up and slow down for the next two years all the way up to 2015. My check went from $500 to $800, to $150 to $300. When President Obama started bringing home the troops, our work slowed down. By this time, I had been at Manchester Federal Prison for eight years.

I knew I was changing because all this time, not once had I been to the hole ("confinement"). I had a few incidents that could have gotten me in the hole. I always thanked Allah for that. I guess I could say he knew I was trying my best to stay out of trouble. One of the reasons for me staying out of trouble was my job in Unicor. You would lose your job for 6-months and up to a year. It all depended on what kind of write up you had. And because I was on a dollar-a-ticket job, where dudes were lining up to take my place. So even if I got my job back after getting out of the hole. I would still have to wait for my operation to come back open.

One of the pressures of working in Unicor was every time there was a big issue in the prison between inmates and staff, all the non-Unicor workers would expect everyone to set it off by laying down and not go to work. I remember the first time one of these situations came up. I wasn't really feeling it because it was about staff taking away late night TV privileges. They used to let us stay in the TV room until 12 AM every night. The reason I didn't care was because I went to bed at 10 PM. Being a convict and on real nigga time, I had to ride with the majority. But every time it was time to lay down, the majority would turn into the minority. The guys that were doing the most talking to promote the lay down would be the first to fall back off the front line. When things looked like you had to take one for the team and go to the hole they wanted us to lose our job for the TV.

I know enough from reading books like *Up the River* and the *New Jim Crow* that us working in the Unicor factory was playing right into the hands of the Powers that Be. Dudes that didn't work in Unicor would say things like, y'all just working to keep ya'll self in prison. They were right in a way. Because if we had a nationwide set down and refused to work the factories, the Feds, and their investors would lose money and have no reason to keep us locked up for so long. They knew that would never happen because the inmates were too divided amongst each other, no unity. And that's what it takes to fight against the Feds, unity amongst the people. What sense did it make for us to be the only prison in the B.O.P. to lay down against Unicor. When all they would do is back the bus up and exchange us for another group of inmates. Every time we stood up for change, I would always call a town hall meeting and say as much. The way I used to deal with changes like things being taken away from us was I would never get us to anything at all. Not the TV microwave, phone, etc. The one thing I cared about other than my job was the weights. I loved to work out with the iron. Unicor always ate first, so on the weekend when we had overtime, it gave me the chance to be first at the weights which led me to the next part of this story.

It would be the love for the weight pile that would trigger a chain of events that would almost cost me my life, and set off one of the worst race riots in Manchester history. To be totally truthful, it really started in Unicor, but it ended up jumping off on the rec yard. Before I go into detail on what happened on the weight pile, let me take you back two months before. You remember I told you that the Sureno Mexican gang had all the Q.A. jobs in the factory? Because of the downsizing of the war and President Obama pulling the troops back home, our work had slowed down, so the factory management took away the ticket pay. Then they changed the way the factory operated. Instead of four sections, they combined the sections to make two long lines. There weren't enough jobs for everybody so they picked the best workers out of each station to make up the two lines.

The factory went from 600 people to 300, and only 100 of them were straight pay jobs. What they did was make the guys on the line be paid in group pay. I was so good at sewing, they made me a straight pay grade one-line leader. The job came with a lot of responsibilities. I had to train new guys on operation and fix rework so the line could keep moving. This was how I kept bumping heads with the Surenos Q.A. It was their job to check the line work. The only reason they used to let most of our work pass was because some of their guys were on the line working as well. Their money was tied in with the rest of the line. Being a line leader I had guys depending on me to help them push the bundles into the finish box, so they could make some money for that day. The Q.A.s and us line leaders were going to get paid because we were all straight pay. The thing with the Surenos was that they would not make a move without the shot caller's approval. I was into it with the head man for the Surenos on the yard. It was only a matter of time and opportunity before he made a move on me. I was checking him on a daily basis. I was not making him look good in front of his guys. A part of me wanted him to jump out there so I could punish him. I didn't have any respect for him because he did a lot of bullshit just cause! What really had me mad was how a lot of the black dudes would bow down to the Mexican gangs. Then when a dude like me stood up to them, niggas would run around talking behind my back making it seem like I was starting the problem with the Mexicans.

I already made up my mind that if it ever came down to war with these Surenos, I would go hard and not look for any help from a lot of these dudes. I wasn't the only dude who was seeing the moves the Surenos were making around the yard. Slowly but surely, they had been putting claims on whatever they felt like had any value. It had started way back when they first hit the compound. It wasn't but a handful of them. Back in 2010, they made a push on the New York boy's table in the chow hall. They had all the support of another Mexican gang, the Paisas. But they still didn't have enough numbers. Then, when they saw that most of the black cars came out to stand with the New York boys, they backed off. Then a year later we were at a standoff with them over a TV situation in one of the units. There numbers were growing and the niggas they had beef with came to an agreement to share the TV which later they lost altogether to the same Sureno.

The one thing I give them credit for is they are real patient. They bide their time just right. They were putting down their stamp in the Food Service, inside ground, and on the rec yard. They had their handball court and pool table. I knew they were making a play for the weight pile. It took them a long time to pull the shit they had been slowly working on with the weights. As we lost real niggas that was helping hold the weight pile down, the more it fell on me and a few more other real niggas. We lost Big Ponique, Big Psyche from Ohio, and Bone from Detroit. That left me and my Muslim brother Mel ("Jamal") from Ohio. Bro had the weight pile on lock for real. I would hold it down after dinner. He kept the peace. He even kept me in line because he had to stop me from blowing up the yard more than once over the weight pile, But when he left, I really felt like I was on my own trying to keep the slot open for the black cars to have weights to work out with.

It was getting bad. You had dumb niggas paying the Surenos to use the weights. When I heard about that, I knew then I had to just worry about me and my car's weights. Everybody knew you had to show me that paperwork to work out with me or get in line for my weights. So you had a lot of hot rat ass niggas buying weights to keep from showing paperwork. Then, I relaxed on my rule this one time because my Muslim brother named 30 had this nigga he was in the unit with named Country Black from Chattanooga work out with us. I found out later the hard way this nigga was hot (a rat). That brings me to how I almost lost my life and caused the compound to go up in a race riot.

CHAPTER THREE

"Green Light"

Being in the same spot for eight years you get used to a routine. The convict word for routine is *biding*. Once you get set in doing your bid. It's on you to make sure everybody else respects the lane you are in. It could be a little thing like where you put your chair in the TV area. If you make a claim to something and you value it, you have to be able to hold it down. Then you have all the different cars and races making claims for things that are supposed to be for the use of everybody. To keep the peace on the yard, a lot of things are broken down by race.

In the units they gave us nine televisions. The Spanish had two TVs, the whites had one, the blacks had three. Then you had the Sports TV, the News TV, and the Movie TV. That's how we had it worked on my unit. But every unit was different according to who had the numbers and control over that unit. When it came to the TVs, I didn't have much need for it. But I still understand the importance of holding down what belongs to the Muslims first, and the blacks. Not because I was racist, it wasn't anything like that. It was just about making sure brothers that came after me had something and that was the mindset of all the cars. It was just an unwritten code of convicts. I watched my unit flip a few times, but for the most part it kept some real niggas and we always had a lot of Muslims on the block. We kept the Iman on my block as well. Now it was Amin ("Stacy Busby") from D.C. He wasn't but 5'6", but had the heart of a 6'4" dude. Cool as hell but don't get on his bad side, he would push that iron. All over the compound the climate had changed for the worst. If you was a real nigga, they even had a group of hot niggas that clicked up out the Midwest and told their homies they weren't going anywhere. If somebody tried to run them up, they were going with them; meaning they were standing their ground. It ended up being a few fights behind that stand, but the hot niggas were still on the yard. They had a section in the chow hall now on the white side.

The Surenos car had grown. They moved to the New York table after all since the real niggas had left. Then they took over a few tables from the whites. They were making moves all over. They had the cigarette game on lock. They even had one night a week on a non-Spanish TV in my unit to watch Gangland on Wednesday. I saw things heading out of control with them and I was constantly pointing out to whoever would listen. Me and some of the old heads could see the moves the Surenos were making. To keep it all the way 100% it was because of them that the gang formed a coalition. The Surenos formed a coalition with the Paisas. To give you a clear picture of what they were doing, I'll tell you a story of how petty and thirsty these Sureno guys were getting.

During every meal, the C.O.s would line up in two lines, and when an inmate exited the chow hall we would have to walk in between the two lines. They would randomly pick an inmate to pat search   and when they found food that you   was trying to steal out the chow hall they would throw it in the garbage right next to the chow hall. They would find packages of vegetables, meats, eggs, even milk. All these items were for   sell on the compound. For a long time, whoever had the job on the inside compound detail would recover the packages from the garbage bin. They had it worked out with each other to split the money made off the bin. Then here came the Surenos, they two of their guys on the detail and made a play for the garbage bin. There was only one black still working on the detail. He was from Ohio. He was cool with a few of my Ohio Muslim brothers, so he stepped to them for back up. That's how I got aware of the situation.

The brothers stepped to the Sureno   shotcaller and they ended up working out a deal with them. But I was on the front line, meaning mugging the shot caller. He knew I wanted some smoke with them. It was an inner conflict because I was trying to change my old ways. I just didn't like how they were making claims on every little thing and getting away with it. I found out what the deal was, anything the C.O. took away from a Mexican, the Sureno guy would get and the Ohio brother could get whatever else. My Muslim brother said that was fair to keep the peace and not drag the community into war with the Surenos. The more they made power moves like that, it was giving them an inch. They wanted a yard. And as their numbers grew the more claims they made. It reminded me of how a dog pisses on his territory for every peace negotiated to them, that was a win. They took it as being feared. I felt like I was the only one paying attention to that fact.

Then came the clash between the D.C. boys and Knoxville car. The Tennessee car was broken up by cities: Nashville, Knoxville, and Chattanooga. There weren't a lot of dudes from Memphis and there were a few G.D.s and Vice Lords on count, so Knoxville was on their own when it came to the rumble on the basketball court with the D.C. boys. I hate that I wasn't out there that day because I felt like I could have prevented it from going down or at least tried.

One of the head D.C. dudes in the mix that day was my Muslim brother Smoke. He was a real nigga serious about that paperwork. That's how we became close as brothers. Smoke kept a banger on him at all times and the D.C. homies that hung around him did too. I knew for a fact they did, and they were ready for work all the time. I don't know why the Knoxville dudes even played basketball with them that day. Everybody on the compound knew them D.C. boys play a different kind of basketball. We gave it a name: D.C. Ball! I used to watch them play on the weekend in the gym against themselves, and it was like watching U.F.C. with a ball. No cap! And they didn't believe in making calls for fouls. They just fouled the one who fouled them harder. But that day on the yard, it started with one of the niggas I was cool with from Knoxville named Charlie, and one of the young D.C. dudes over a foul call.

Charlie was a wild nigga too. I knew him from Blunt County Jail. From what I heard, Charlie and this nigga from Knoxville named Smiley was the only two Knoxville dudes fighting back. They say the rest of the K-Town dudes that were out there ran and left some of their homies getting crushed. One of their homies named George got stabbed up in the chest while his main man watched and ran on him. The yard got shut down. They shipped Smoke and a group of the D.C. boys. Charlie, Smiley and George got transferred too. A lot of the cars had issues with the D.C. boys for one reason: They were wild.

I was used to being around niggas that was turned up and on "Go" all the time. They reminded me of the way I used to rock with my homies in the state pen. Putting pressure on the yard made some niggas fold and some harden up. But when it came down to dealing with the Surenos, I rather have the D.C. boys on my side because they were going to push that iron no question about it. So when the car took that hit because of the rumble on the basketball court, they lost numbers and some real hitters at that. It tilted in the Surenos' favor because the D.C. boys, like it or not, were a help keeping the Surenos in check. A lot of dudes wouldn't want to admit it, but I knew it was a fact on the yard. I was paying attention to how aggressive the Sureno swag had gotten from before. Withhe loss of Smoke and his crew, we were losing real niggas left and right. I was becoming the front line advocate against the Surenos push for more territory on the compound.

I knew word was getting back to their shot caller about me. I was smart enough to know didn't nobody keep secrets in prison. Men can be worse than women at gossiping. I didn't really care, it wasn't like I was scared of them. I was just trying to wake as many brothers up to what was happening right before their eyes. We were losing control of the yard and it seemed like nobody but me and a few old heads cared. But I knew what the real problem was. The Mexicans were more organized. Their structure was more disciplined. They had unity. They kept their car clean of rats. While at least ratting on each other, because they had a rule that it was alright to snitch on blacks, but never on your homie.

We had two major problems as far as I could see. One, there was no real unity amongst the black cars. Then some of the black cars were cuffing hot niggas (rats). And as we got into the year of 2015 on Manchester yard we were heading into a transformation period. The Mexican gangs were getting stronger and the yard was turning over from real to rats. Don't get me wrong, there was still a lot of real niggas on the yard. The thing was getting them to see what was happening. The TV and the garbage bin incident or the move on the New York tables weren't enough to convince any of the black cars that the Surenos were trying to suck up the yard. They were going to wait too late and before we knew it, nothing would be ours.

During this time, I was going through bad times with my on-again, off-again girlfriend. I wasn't getting any visits so I spent my weekends working overtime in the factory or working out on the weight pile. My weekend slot on the weight pile was from 7:30 AM – 10:30 AM, which was the first rec move until the yard closed. But if we had overtime, I would miss lunch and use that hour to workout. On the weight pile things were broken up into slots for different cars to use the weights. All races had cars that used the weights to workout. It was over a couple thousand pounds of iron on the weight pile. At any given time, there would be maybe 6-8 cars working out at the same time.

The white boys were the smallest percent of people on the pile and they got the least amount of weight. I was just about even with the black and Spanish cars. Some slots the blacks would have more, other times it would be the Spanish boys. An unwritten rule was when a car passes down the weight, they leave it with their race. That way things stay fair. But leave it to somebody to try to have all the sense and take more weight than they were supposed to have.

The Rec Orderly would set the weights up near the station, and when the cars came out to the pile, they go to the station to grab the weights they would use for that day. This system, when respected by everybody kept the peace. Every once in a while we would have to explain it to a new lone wolf, that is a new dude without a car, that thinks it was just free weights for everybody. Every race was responsible for explaining this to their people.

Being that I was one of the old timers on the weight pile, and because I spent my whole rec time on the weight pile I did not play. When I went to the yard, I didn't play sports or kick it with the homies or anything like that. It was all workout, weight pile, nowhere else. So on my slot, I knew who got what and where they worked out. I had the respect of everybody except a few Mexicans. That was because of the new leadership of the Surenos. I was in his way of taking over the weight pile. They were already selling a portion of their weight to whoever would buy it. And that was starting problems because you would have extra people on the weight pile with weight and no station to use it on. The thing that pissed me off the most was their real presence on the weight pile was not to work out. They wanted to control for profit and influence. In the past I had to check one of their homies over some weight he thought belonged to them. I actually put hands on dude, and if it wasn't for my Muslim brother Mel from Ohio stepping in between us, I was about to knock him out. The fact that I mushed him in the face was enough of a violation of the hands-off policy to send us to war with the Surenos. They had a different shot caller at the time. And their numbers weren't right for war then. Mel had a real good understanding with their shot caller at that time. They both worked on the yard together. But bro was upset with me for losing my temper and mushing dude. He gave me a big homie talk with some Islamic advice and that chilled me out for a while.

I was building up green light points with the enemy. I know I was at the top of their list, but they were at the top of mine too. Mainly the head man, the shot caller was in my crosshairs. I wasn't hiding the fact that I didn't care for him and anytime he wanted to become a real man and test his hand I was ready for war! He wasn't dumb at all. He had patience and was biding his time for a hit on me. After the rumble with the Tennessee and D.C. boys, I could tell the Sureno was feeling stronger on the yard. They were doing all kinds of bold moves in the units and in Unicor.

In one of the units they took another TV. It was Unit C-A. In Unicor, me and the other line leader was constantly in arguments trying to get them to put the work in the box so the line could get paid. Not knowing to me and at the time, but their shot caller had already put a green light on me. A green light in Federal prison was a kill hit put on you by a car to all its members. They were just waiting for me to be in the right spot under the right condition. They knew on the compound I was a well loved and respected O.G. by all the real niggas in every car. And on top of all that, I'm Muslim, and we had one of the biggest cars on the pound. Their shot caller had to know hitting me would mean a war. But I guess he was willing to deal with the consequences. It would be nature that would set the chain of events off. That led up to me being stabbed eight times and air lifted to the outside hospital.

It was a Saturday morning. I woke up at 6:00 AM. Five minutes before my cell door was open by the C.O. I always made sure I beat my door open. An open door with a sleeping body gives opportunity to your enemy. So I always stayed on point. I was on point that morning. I offered my Salat prayer after washing up. Then I stepped out of my cell to make myself a cup of coffee, ate a banana and a granola bar. That's when I heard someone say, "Damn, it's fog count."

I walked to the window to see for myself. Yeah, there it was a sea of white, covering the whole compound. A person couldn't see two steps in front of them. The fog count on the weekend pushes everything back when it comes to movement. It holds up people's visits with their families. It stops the morning rec move. When this happens, there is nothing to do but go eat breakfast or go back to your cell and lay back. That's what I did. My celly was still asleep. He was my little Muslim brother Jabreel from D.C. He was a real youngster, 20 years old and cool as hell and kept me laughing at his days on boat (aka PCP or "water"). Nevertheless, the fog count normally lasted until 12:00 PM. I had it worked out with some of my work out crew about the weights. We had to miss lunch and would only get 45 minutes to an hour to use the weights, or however long they take to feed lunch. So that's what was happening that day.

After the fog count, me and 30 (my Muslim brother) and Country Black, from Tennessee, made our way to the weight pile. I could tell right away that it was going to take them a while to feed lunch because not that many people were in the rec yard. The basketball courts were full with two teams of players. It looked like it was some G.D.s playing some dudes from Kentucky. I couldn't really tell, it could have been another unit, who knows? All I know was where all the blacks were posted up at. I always paid attention to who was on the yard. I didn't want to walk into nobody else's beef. The yard was mostly Mexican on the handball courts and in the weight pile with me. I didn't think too much into the numbers because I was never scared to walk the yard no matter what. I'm a trained warrior when it comes to combat. And on the weight pile there were too many weapons at hand. Altogether there were 9 blacks on the weight pile. That was counting my crew of three plus this dude from Kentucky. Four of them were out of the workout crew and two dudes from Tennessee. The rest were Surenos; two crews made up of eight.

It was our chest day so we needed to use a flat bench. This was what had started the whole conflict. Being it wasn't our normal slot time, we had an agreement with the Surenos to use the flat bench station until their people came on the rec yard after chow. In the past it was never a problem. But now today the so-called shot caller wanted to make an issue out of it. There was nobody using the flat bench, but because it was me asking out of respect for the system we all agreed to. He wanted to pull a power ego move on me and told us we couldn't use it.

I couldn't believe he was trying me like that! I got mad instantly. *Who the fuck this little bitch ass nigga think he was talking to?"* That was the thought going through my mind as I kept a straight face and tried reasoning with him. I told him we wouldn't take long. All we wanted was a few sets and would be done. He wasn't trying to hear anything I was saying. I could see the pleasure all on his face for holding my workout up and me having to ask him to use the bench. My patience was growing short because the time I was spending talking to him was eating up my workout time. The other black cars on the pile stopped working out when they heard my voice starting to raise. We were in a little standoff. My crew, 30 and Black, and the Sureno shot caller with his homies all around the bench I wanted to use. He was standing right next to it like he was protecting it from me. One of the guys in the Kentucky crew offered to let us get their flat bench. Then this scary ass nigga from Knoxville, Tennessee kept trying to get me to back down. I could tell the other black dudes other than 30, my Muslim brother, was scared I was going to push off and set it off right there. So I went to the shot caller differently. I asked him if he had something against me personally and if so let me and him handle it one on one. He jumped on the defense trying to save face in front of his boys by saying he was a Sureno and they don't do one on one. So I told him what I thought about that statement.

I said, "The only reason ya'll don't do one on one is because y'all cowards and can't fight."

You should have seen the look on their faces. Priceless. They knew they were fighting words. And if they didn't address it right then, the word would get out how I checked them in front of their shot caller.

They would lose respect from their own people. I knew what the hell I just did. I forced their hand. And the shot caller knew too, because he wasn't smiling and played it cool now. He was thinking real hard on his next move. He couldn't let me get away with disrespecting him in front of his homies. But he was looking at me and I could tell he saw I was ready for whatever. What he didn't know about me, was that I'm trained to go! I'm really about that life, and I wanted some smoke. The other niggas around me, other than 30, was talking up trying to ease the tension. But it was too late. I had put the ball in the Sureno's court. When I saw that the shot caller wasn't ready for no smoke, and I was tired of hearing this Tennessee nigga beg me to let it go. I just snapped and told the nigga they were soft, and they can let the Mexicans have the weight pile. I was done trying to make weak niggas strong.

I told 30 and Black that I was done for today. I wasn't going to work out with these soft ass niggas watching my back. We left the weight pile. I was so mad I told 30 and Black let's walk a lap around the track. We couldn't leave the rec yard until the next move anyway. And that wouldn't be until after they were done feeding chow. I knew 30 was just as mad as I was. He loved to work out. He was ready to push if I said so. I couldn't tell how Black was taking all this. He didn't say anything the whole time I was checking the Sureno. I didn't know much about Black other than he was from Tennessee and strong as hell. That's why I didn't really mind when 30 brought him to the crew. But I should've still checked his work.

We passed the niggas on the basketball court. A couple of them spoke to me wondering why I wasn't working out. I told one of the G.D.s, a young nigga I was cool with to be on point because I had just checked the Sureno shot caller on the weight pile. We made a full lap and then we stopped and sat on the wall near the baseball field. On our way around the track, I kept my eye on all the movements the Sureno Mexicans were making. They were in one big huddle on the handball court. I told 30 that they looked like they were up to something. He felt the same. I showed him the bats lying on the softball field. We agreed to get near them. That's why we were sitting where we were when a group of Surenos started walking our way.

I didn't take off for the bats right away because I didn't know what was on their mind yet. And I didn't want to look scared. So as they got near, the shot caller called out to me like he just wanted to talk peace. He was a real smooth talker, and would fool you if you didn't know who he was. I walked over to him and two of his homies. I wasn't scared. I knew I could handle at least two of them by myself. No cap. One of the three was kind of cool with me in a respectful way. He had been on the compound longer than the shot caller and the other Surenos. Seeing him was one of the reasons I let my guard down. He was one of the Surenos that was always trying to keep the peace. It was really him who I had the fog deal with on the weight pile.

It was a deal we had for years, way before this sucka ass shot caller they had now running the car. Peace maker Sureno jumped on the scorer's tower for the softball field. That left me and the shot caller and his other homie on the ground. There was a group of them hanging back from us. I didn't pay them too much attention. The little shot caller started talking real cool, calm and collected. He was saying that I shouldn't have called him a coward and he wasn't scared to fight. But it was just how his gang got down. A whole bunch of the same old shit he was saying on the weight pile. Only now it seemed like he was explaining to me more than telling me in a hard way. It felt peaceful, let's squash the beef talk. So, I tried to help him by making it easy and said I was wrong for calling them cowards.

"But none of this would have happened if you would have kept the deal me and your homies have been doing for years."

Then he fucked up the whole peace talk by saying his man didn't have the right to work out a deal with nobody without his say so. That's when I felt myself getting aggravated with him all over again. He really thought he was this big boss on the yard. The conversation started going left. He said something I didn't like, I said something back. Then his homeboy started moving in front of me to my left side. So I stepped over to keep him in eyesight. That's when I caught the shot caller lunging at me as if to hit me in the face. I pulled my head back to weave the blow.

I did, but he caught me in the chest. He was never aiming at my face from the jump; it was a stab move to the chest. I had my water cooler in my right hand, so I swung it at him catching him in the left ear. The water jug bust over his head. At the same time, his homie stuck me in the back of my neck with the banger he had. I was in battle mode now. And I couldn't feel any of the stab wounds that were punched into me by these two. I hit the Sureno's homeboy who had stuck me in the neck with a hook that sent him into the softball field gate. That bought me a minute with him, but the shot caller was fast this time hitting me four more times in the chest with his banger.

I was leaking real bad now, but I couldn't afford to stop fighting now. I was wondering where 30 and Black were? Could they see? I didn't see what was happening to me. I opened up a flurry of punches on the shot caller knocking him down to the ground. I was going to stump him out but his homie hit me in the back arm with the banger reminding me that they had weapons. I thought about the first plan: The bats on the field. So I took off running to where I had seen them laying on the field, and to my surprise one of the Surenos had beat me to it. So I hit the brakes in mid-stride. When I turned to change direction towards the basketball courts, I felt a sharp pain in my side. When looked down at my side I noticed the blood blood all over my white tee shirt. All at once I started feeling the pain from all the stab wounds.

Next was shortness of breath that made me drop to one knee. I almost made it to the basketball court, but I was close enough for the young niggas out there to see me. I heard someone call out asking if I was okay. I think it was the same GD young nigga I had given the heads up to when me, 30 and Black were walking the track. I couldn't answer him because I was having a hard time breathing. So I just shook my head. No, they all stopped playing basketball. By now I know they had finally figured out that we were into it with the Mexicans.

A couple guys came to help me up. As they were lifting me up, I looked around to see a sea of C.O.s and white shirt officers. They had hit the "deuces." The alert had sent all officers on deck charging. When that happens every inmate is supposed to take a knee. So by the guys having me propped up walking me the C.O.s were drawn to what was going on. When they got close and saw all the blood on my shirt, I could hear one of them calling for medical on the radio for a medical emergency in the rec yard. Then all I heard after that was questions.

"What happened?"

"Where are you hurt?"

"Can you walk on your own?"

"Who did this to you?"

I never answered. I just closed my eyes a little bit and passed out. But I wasn't gone. I could still see. The C.O.s started bustling orders to everybody around telling dudes to move over there, stay there, clear the way for medical staff. They came rushing in the gate. We had made it out the grass and onto the sidewalk coming from the track. They had a wheelchair for me. I sat down in it and they wheeled me right past the Surenos.

There they were kneeling down in a group. We had to go right past them with their shit eating grins on their faces. Like they were the only ones who knew the joke, and it was on me! I wasn't worried about them doing nothing while so many C.O.s were there. But I was the one fighting with myself not to try to kick their grins off every one of them, but my body won that fight because it couldn't do what my brain wanted it to do. As they were rolling me to medical, I noticed guys running out the open door to the units. Word was spreading about the hit on me by the Surenos.

Because of the blood loss, I was starting to feel weak. Then came the coughs with me spitting up blood. The nurse told another nurse that my lung had been punctured. I can't lie, I was getting scared. When I heard my lung was hurt, shit started sounding real serious to me. I didn't know they stabbed me that deep. The head nurse told the Lieutenants and officers that they would have to call for an ambulance for me. As the nurse was talking to the LT, his radio was blowing up with the deuces. All officers to Whitley (A) — that was my unit. Then another call for all staff to report to Clay A unit.

From the sound of things, it had popped off out there. The first thought that came to my mind was my Muslim brothers done greenlighted the Sureno. My confirmation came in the form of unconscious Mexicans laid out on stretchers. The first two Mexicans that came into the medical were so fucked up. One had a smashed in head. He was laid out unconscious. The other one was bleeding from the head and from stab wounds. They were worse off than me, so they ended up taking my ambulance away twice. I remember hoping that one of my guys got the head shot caller.

Medical was filling up real fast. They had started putting dudes into the holding cell. They had me in the hallway still in the wheelchair. I was glad they didn't handcuff me like they were doing everybody else they brought in. I guess they forgot to do me. However, I was glad. I didn't want an enemy to come in and I couldn't protect myself. They came in with 30 in handcuffs. He had been stabbed too, but not bad. So they were taking him straight to the hole. My ambulance came and I was taken to the outside hospital.

I wound up staying in the hospital for a week. They did surgery on my lung. I had to have a breathing tube. The doctor told me it was good that I was built up like I was with muscle in my chest. It stopped the weapons from reaching my heart. I felt blessed lying in that hospital bed. I humbled myself, thanking Allah for sparing my life. I made him another promise, that I would stop walking around with my shirt off and my chest stuck out making enemies. But instead I would change and start acting like my Muslim name; Shahid which means "Witness of Allah." I would do things that call people to Islam instead of becoming enemies. I felt bad that the brother had to push off because of my short temper. I still had a lot of work to do with working on myself. So, when I got released from the hospital they put me in the hole. I was still in pain from the surgery. They went in through a small hole beneath my navel.

I was on pain pills because the stab wounds still had scar tissue. It's hard to describe the pain. It was an irritable burning feeling. The doctor told me it could take months for my injury to fully heal because of how deep they were. Back in prison, when they put me in confinement, the staff had split the hole up with each wing holding black inmates or Mexican inmates. I was put in the cell with the Iman, Amin aka Stacy Bugby from D.C.

When they popped the cell door, my brother Iman was smiling and happy to see me. I smiled back and then I gave him his right by Salaming him. "As salamu Alakum Ahki."

He gave me the greeting back. He was about to step in and give me a brotherly hug when I put my hand in front to halt him, reminding him of my injury. As the C.O. closing the cell door behind me, I could hear the whole wing come alive with my guys, mostly from my unit, calling my name.

"Yo, Miami!"

"Miami, what's good?"

"Miami, you alright, homie!"

"Miami, we broke them off for you!"

"Miami, I went the hardest, cuz!"

I knew right away who all the voices were. That last one with the "cuz" was a wild ass Crip King named Celo from Nashville, Tennessee. Then it was D2. He was from Nashville too, 52 Crip. Sunny from Ohio was another one of my Muslim brothers. I know I heard Jabeer's voice too, he was my celly from D.C. The wing was full of guys out of my unit. I felt honored for the love and ashamed because they were all here because of me. Real good dudes, solid dudes, souljas riding for my cause.

We were close together in the holding cells. As long as we talked one at a time everybody could hear what was being said. As soon as I got settled in, the stories started up. Everybody on the wing wanted to let me know what went down in the unit and on the compound after I got stabbed. My young celly went first with his version of how things popped off in the unit. He was one of the first guys to make it back to the unit with the news of me being stabbed. I didn't even know he was out there in the rec yard that day. But come to find out, he was in the pool room playing pool when it happened. So, according to him when the C.O. hit the deuces, they came on the yard and left the door leading to the compound open. So him and all the dudes ran off the yard back to the units. He had already seen me being put into the wheelchair. So he took off running to let Amin know what happened. That's when Amin jumped in the story and took it from there. He was right in the cell with me, but he was talking loud enough for everybody else to hear. He said "Jabeer" came to the door yelling his name saying "Amin, they stabbed Shaheed!!"

He kept saying it over and over. Like it didn't happen or it wasn't real. Amin grabbed him to slow him down and to hear what the hell he was talking about. As Jabeer was telling Amin what he knew, noticed the Mexicans in the unit grouping up in the back of the unit. They got the news at the same time and were preparing themselves for the backlash. Amin went into war mode calling all the Muslims on the block together. Him and Tank went to where we kept our bangers on the unit.

He made me laugh at this part of the story. We had our bangers hiding in the wall of one of our Muslim cells. We were letting a dude from Kentucky live there. When Tank and Amin ran into the cell, the dude was surprised to see those bangers coming out the wall in their cell. I could only imagine the look on their faces. Coming out of the cell, Amin was met by Celo and Dee2. They were both bangered up. By now the unit was split by race. The Mexicans were all in one corner. The white boys and whoever didn't want to be involved in the war that was about to take place went to their cells. All eyes were on Amin. The real niggas in the unit were ready to ride. But they wanted the Muslims to set the war off because I was in their car.

Amin led the charge with the Muslim front. Those who didn't have a banger had broom sticks, pipes, and locks in socks. Amin asked the Mexican to step aside and let him talk to the Sureno that was in the unit. There were only two known Surenos in our unit, Bug Head and Louie. But the Paisa Mexican wanted to protect them, so when he refused Amin's request, Amin gave Sonny the Go Head nod. That's when Sonny took off with the broomstick and all hell broke loose.

Niggas started swinging and grabbing Mexicans and beating them to sleep. There were some Mexicans ready for war themselves. They had bangers and some were throwing scalding hot water they had microwaved beyond steaming. That's why they chose the corner by the microwave. One thing I can say about them Mexicans, they're very smart when it comes to being creative.

One on Muslim brothers name Naji, from the Middle East, got hit in the head with a lock by one of the new black dudes in the unit that mistook Naji for a Mexican. Another one of my Muslim brothers named Buda had to save Naji. Celo got cornered in one of the top tiers by a group of Mexicans. So he had to jump to get away. My celly and his homie from D.C. named Tank were Muslims, and they resorted to throwing books, shoes, whatever else they could lay their hands on. Two of the biggest black dudes in the unit were from Ohio and they were dropping Mexicans left and right bare handed.

We stayed up all night talking. They each told me what happened in the unit. Then I shared my story of how it all got started. Out of respect to them I kept it 100%. Not making it favor my point of view. I told them how I walked away from the weight pile and how I felt like the dude on the weight pile was scared. I let them know I knew when I called them cowards that I had pushed them into a corner where they had to do something to save face. But when they didn't make their move on the weight pile I thought it was over. But I was wrong and they caught me slipping. Making me think they wanted to talk peace. After we called it a night on the stories, me and Amin talked some more just between us. I got much respect for Amin. He is a couple years older than me and very knowledgeable in our religion. e had been down for 17 years now. He had about 60 years, but he was always fighting his case trying to give some time back. That's one reason I was feeling like shit for having everybody in the hole cause of me.

Amin had just got hired in the commissary store. It was one of the best jobs on the compound and one of the hardest to get. He also had a brother working on his case for him. He wasn't the only one back there that sacrificed good jobs and was working towards regaining their freedom. One of the brothers was the head staff cook, which was a good paying job plus a side hustle. A few other of the real niggas that went out for me worked in Unicor with good paying positions. Celo had a football gambling ticket on the yard that was making him a nice bag! It was a whole list of things guys had lost because of me. I felt like real shit thinking about all that made me lay awake all night. I couldn't really sleep anyway. The pain from my injury was hurting as well. They had not written any of us up yet, so that was on all our minds. A write up is like catching a case. But the only difference is, the write up is for the prison to handle, not the courts. We could lose good days. That was the worst part of a write up. Because good days helped us get out of prison early. On top of lost good days, they gave us hole time (locked down for 23 hours a day; 24 hours on weekends) . We could also lose privileges like commissary, visits, phone, and email. With the type of write up we were looking at, meant a transfer. In the Feds you could be sent anywhere in the country. There was nothing to do now but wait and see what the staff had up their sleeves.

They had the whole prison on lockdown because this was race related. It could be weeks on lockdown. Word on inmate.com was that the gangs wanted to keep pushing on the Mexicans. We were all classified under investigation by the warden. That meant they were still trying to figure out what started the riot. Nobody was talking on either side. Me and Amin both agreed that silence wouldn't last long. There were too many snitches on the compound. I thought about who all was out there on the weight pile that knew what really started the war. I knew this one dude who was a real live rat. If anybody was to tell what went down it would be him. He was one of the same niggas I snapped on before I walked off the pile. He was soft as hell and loved to hide behind the Bible with that Christian role he was playing. Don't get me wrong, I have nothing against a real Christian, but I feel like if you are a real man of faith and a Christian, why would you snitch on your people and bring them into your misery? Why didn't you just take your time like a man of faith and trust in God to deliver you out of your hardship?

As a Muslim, I did. I took my time and then asked Allah to not let me do it all. I didn't lie or snitch on anybody because I had faith and belief in God. Nevertheless, being under investigation could last up to six months. They would have to tell us something or let us go! However, we already knew how this was going to play out. At least Amin knew more than me. This was my first time in the hole on the Fed level. Amin said give it a day or two and they started pulling us out one by one for interviews. They were waiting for me to come back from the hospital. That alone let us know they knew some of what happened already. Just as Amin predicted, the very next morning the Captain and Lieutenant over investigation (known as the S.I.S. Officer) came to our wing calling names. Then pulling us out one by one. After the first person came back from the interview we knew what questions they were asking each of us. Knowing that gave us an idea of what they already knew. All this was just format. So they have paperwork showing they did their part. All the real problem solving came when they let us set up a pow wow to politic it out.

In prison, no matter what the situation is, it's always the inmates that do the work. The staff is there to make sure it gets done. As they were pulling us out of the wing there were some more C.O.'s pulling the Mexicans out for interviews on their wing. The interview process went on for two days. After they were done, the S.I.S. officers came back with a cut list. They let out my Muslim brother Naji, the one from the Middle East who got mistakenly hit in the head with a lock. They also freed another one of my Muslim brothers. He was the head staff cook. We all joked with him on his way out, telling him to put a word into his boss. Because we knew he had big pull amongst the staff. They were the only two that got released on our wing. But word got back to us on inmate.com that they cut about 10-15 Mexicans lose. Amin said that was because it was harder to transfer Mexicans because they can't walk every yard. That call was coming from higher up, like the Region.

See Manchester was a Sureno yard amongst the Mexican gangs in the B.O.P.

The Mexican gang situation was different from how the black gangs operate in the system. They didn't allow other rival gangs to be on the same compound as them. So that made it hard for the B.O.P. staff to place them anywhere. So because of that, most of the blacks in our group would be transferred. The next step in their investigation came a week later. They let us and the rest of the compound stay on lockdown for a week to think about how we wanted to play this out. This gave everybody time to think about how they felt about the whole situation. The S.I.S. came to see me.

He was trying to figure out who I really was. Well that's how he came at me. He asked me who I was in regards to my affiliation with the gangs. He was having a real hard time understanding why all the gangs were riding with me. I told him I was a Muslim and I guess because I stood for what's right. It made dudes respect me. He wasn't buying that, and he said as much! He went on to tell me how many years he had been working for the B.O.P. and how he had seen it all. And he knew I was one of the shot callers on the yard. Because that's the only way everybody would be down to blow up the yard about me. He was right in a way. I did have big influence amongst the real niggas on the yard. And they were spread out amongst the cars on the yard. I'm one of the real O.G.s with an official stamp that carried weight with the real niggas. My stamp could have you loved or hated, blessed or cursed.

What the Lieutenant didn't understand was that it was a real nigga car that he didn't know existed. That's because real niggas move in silence. The car was built on checking paperwork, and representing your city. And I was the representative from Miami. Iso, what he didn't know I wasn't going to tell him. After he saw he wasn't getting anywhere with me, I was sent back to my cell.

Time kept moving and it was three weeks since I had gotten stabbed, and two weeks since I'd been back from the hospital. They tried a few times to get the compound back open, but feelings were still raw as niggas were salty about the attempt on my life. It wasn't only with the Mexicans, but niggas was beefing with other niggas that didn't push when shit jumped off. Yeah, it was a lot of niggas that ran to their cell, and didn't put in any work. So the real niggas were running them up. Every time the staff tried to let them off lock, I was getting full reports of what was taking place on the yard through inmate.com and even from some of the cooler C.O.s who would work in the hole from time to time.

I was laying back on my bunk after me and Amin had worked out. The cell door just opened out of the blue, and when I looked up I saw the Captain and the S.I.S. Lieutenant. They wanted both of us to come with them. Amin and I were handcuffed and taken to the rec yard. They put us in the cage and a moments later the Sureno shot caller and his right hand homie were placed in the cage right next to us. The Captain took the floor by saying he needed for us to come to some kind of agreement so he could get his prison back running. The Captain let on that the Warden was breathing down his neck to get the compound back running on normal operation, and he couldn't do that if we didn't get our people out there to make peace. I was willing to do whatever I could to help my real niggas come off lockdown. I knew niggas had shit they needed to be taking care of. It had already been over a month. And besides, the motherfuckers I wanted were in the cage next to me. Amin took the lead on the politicking with the Sureno shot caller. He knew I wasn't any good at it. That's why we were where we were now. He knew whatever he stamped I was rocking with and he was the voice of the Muslim car anyway. They called it off and made peace. But now they were asking the Captain for a favor. We wanted to be clear of any write ups and wanted to see how many more of our guys he could let back out. Amin added that he made sure our Ramadan fast would be honored back in the hole. The Captain said he would do what he could and would see about releasing some more of our guys so they could carry the word back to the yard about the peace agreement. He did let us know that there wouldn't be any write ups because his staff also made mistakes that allowed the problem to grow like it did. That made me feel a little better because now with nobody getting written up, we wouldn't lose good days. However, we were still getting transferred. How long would that take? We didn't know.

Me and Amin prepared ourselves to do Ramadan back there in the hole. Ramadan is a holy month in Islam, it is obligatory for every month to fast. Ramadan is one of the pillars of faith in Islam. It's the month when the Holy Book of the Qur'an was revealed to the Prophet Muhammad (PBAH). The way we had to fast was from sun up to sun down, no eating or drinking. It was a time where we were supposed to spend time reflecting on our actions so we could get better in our spiritual walk back to Allah.

Being on lock down in the hole gave me all the time I needed to slow down and really think my life over. Here I was in prison in lock up. I was 40 years old and I was still fucking up. I felt ashamed of myself. There were younger brothers in our community that never got into anything. It had to be me to crash out the Muslim car. I shared how I felt about that with Amin. He gave me some brotherly advice. Then encouraged me to turn to Allah in prayer. That's what I loved about Bro, he was always positive. You wouldn't have guessed he had all that time or how long he had been down by the way he carried himself. That was one reason why he got my vote for leadership over the community.

The first day of Ramadan came, and along with it came peace. Fasting always does that for me. I guess it was because with hunger pains came the remembrance of Allah. Amin helped me learn some new Surahs out the Qur'an in Arabic. As I read my Qur'an daily and meditated on its meanings my heart started to soften. I remember reading this one Surah in the Qur'an Surah 31, it's called Luqman. He was a man that lived a long time ago. In the Chapter in the Qur'an, Luqman gave his son some advice. The advice was about his character and mannerism. He was told not to be loud or arrogant. Not to walk around with your head and chest poked out. Reading these words was like me looking into the mirror at myself. It made me understand why the Sureno shot caller had a grudge with me. It was the arrogant way I presented myself to people. Looking at things that way gave me an understanding of what I needed to do. Allah was showing me that I needed to humble myself. When my next prayer time came in, I asked Allah to forgive me and created in me a humble heart and spirit from that day forward. I began to work on my temper. I became conscious of the way I presented myself to others. To see if I was really serious about changing my attitude, Allah sent me a test in the form of the C.O. Who worked the 4-12 shift in the hole. He was one of those red-bearded white hillbillies out of Kentucky. He was just back from the Gulf War and had a negative attitude towards Muslims.

Here's the problem we had with him. We would have fasted all day long. So when Food Service sent our trays of food over at 8:00 PM for us to break our fast and eat. his Hillbilly would hold our food an hour (or longer) after it had been delivered. It would be good and cold when he finally brought it to us. We would hear other brothers kicking the door and yelling for their food. But Amin and I didn't fall for his trap. We never even let him know it bothered us. He did this for the first week of Ramadan. Every time he would open our flap to give us our trays, I would make sure he heard me say thank you. I was killing him with kindness.

One of the lessons that comes from fasting is patience and learning how to humble yourself. So dealing with this C.O. was a test to see if I was really changing. My kindness worked. The second week into Ramadan, the same C.O. started bringing our food on time and it was still hot. God was showing me that I didn't have to meet aggression with aggression. But instead I could practice patience. Me and Amin spent our days reading the Qur'an, sharing street stories about our life and thought we were in prison on lockdown, we both thanked Allah. Our backgrounds were very similar. No father in our life, raised by a single working mom, and the streets. Only difference is Amin didn't come up in and out the system like I did. This was his first time being locked up. But it seemed like he got all his at one time. I couldn't imagine what I would've done if I caught all the time he had. It's safe to say I would've been out of my mind. My mind almost slipped away from me with the 20 years I had. My faith in Allah, and making my prayers daily kept me grounded. The whole time I've been in prison I always fought my case. I made it my business to keep up with the law. There were new cases coming out of the Supreme Court that were helping people. Every time I found one that applied to my case, I would put a pro se motion in. That's a motion you file on your own without the help of a lawyer. The courts hate to grant pro se motions because it would be giving corrections to an inmate. And they never want to encourage us to fight our own case.

Outside learning more about my religion, studying the law was my other passion. I had to find it funny when guys came to me for advice on their case. Who would have thought that I would become a jailhouse lawyer? But looking back, knowing it made perfectly good sense for me to have some understanding of how the law system worked. All the years I spent inside this system. We were in the third week of Ramadan, when our Case Manager came around and informed us that our transfer had been approved. Before we could get too happy over the news, she also let us know the transfer process would take a few more months, but for some of us it can be a little faster than others. It all depends on where we were designated to. Next, we all asked where we were going. She responded saying that all she does is "submit the paperwork." The final decision was up to the Regional Office in Texas. We all had a prison in mind that we hoped we could get to. But a disciplinary transfer was like rolling dice. You could end up wherever. There was nothing else to do but accept our faith. Being in confinement for months, you had to have a strong mindset. The weak minded dudes would fall in all the traps they lay down and end up getting pepper sprayed and getting their cells stripped down.

When they stripped your cell down, they took away all your clothes and linen. The clothes were replaced with a paper jumpsuit and paper bed linen. This was a form of punishment made for you to freeze from the cold air. They kept the air super cold. It didn't bother me after a week or so in the hole. My body adapted to the conditions. They offered us rec for an hour a day, five days a week. But even that had a catch to it. They ran rec real early in the morning at 7:00 AM when it was cold outside. They also used this opportunity to ransack our cell with a shakedown. The sad part about that was in most cases all they really were looking for was food that we saved off our trays to eat later. They would throw the food away. Some of them would write you up for it. Me and Amin would take turns going to rec. That way at least one of us would be left in the cell at all times. That way they wouldn't come into our cell and mess with the snacks we saved up.

Ramadan came and went. Time was flying for real. It had been over six months since the riot. The compound was back up and running, and we would get word from inmate.com on all the politics going down between the shot callers, G.D.s and Vice Lords. They had run a few of their guys up for not pushing off on the Mexicans when shit jumped off. One of my Muslim brothers put hands on Country Black for running on me and 30 on the rec yard when we were fighting. After all that, everything settled down again. They picked a few of us out every two weeks when the bus came to drop off new inmates. Me, Amin, Cleo, white boy Stutter left the same day. We went to Atlanta to be transferred out to different prisons.

On the bus to Atlanta the transit officer let us know what prison we were designated to. I was headed to Forrest City, Arkansas. That's where they had the rapper T.I. and even Mike Tyson did time there.. They both were at the low-custody prison. I was going to the F.C.I. (medium-security prison). All I could think about was there was no chance of me getting a visit out there in no-Black-Man-Land Arkansas. I told myself that I was going to stay out of trouble for however long they asked me to in order to get transferred. But for right now, I was hoping not to stay too long in Atlanta.

Anybody who has ever been in the Feds will tell you that the Atlanta holdover was the nastiest place in the world. The mats they issued to sleep on were pissy and dirty as hell. The food was terrible. The guards talked to inmates crazy and disrespectful. They kept us on lock down all day. We came out to shower and used the phone for about two hours at the most. I was ready to go after four days down there. Some of the other guys like Cleo and Amin had already left a day after we got there. Me and white boy Stutter were the only ones still waiting. Now I was leaving Stutter too. It was a long ride to Oklahoma. Yeah, they sent me way up there to have to turn around and bring me back to Arkansas. That's how the Feds play when they put you through transit. I really didn't mind telling you the truth. After being on that mountain in Kentucky after eight years in one place, it was a relief to see part of the world again.

I stayed a full month in Oklahoma waiting to go to Forrest City F.C.I. The unit they put me in was full of guys waiting to go to the same place. There were so many of us they put us on a plane then flew us down to Memphis where two buses were waiting on us. From there it was only an hour ride to Forrest City F.C.I., Low, Camp. The prison complex was set in the middle of the rice field. The bus I was on pulled up to the gate of the F.C.I. They drove us into the sally port, unloaded us off into two lines and we had to go through R&D (Receiving and Discharge) to get processed in. That took all of four hours.

They assigned me to C-2, a unit in C Block. My celly was this young brother from Memphis. Everybody called him Jitt. He was cool. We did the paperwork introduction, standing by the real nigga code. Being the O.G., he gave me the bottom bunk out of respect. I dug the young blood from the start. He gave me the rundown on the joint. I told him I was Muslim and I was from Miami. After counting,he showed me who the Muslims were in the unit. There were three brothers in the unit. There was Rashid from Memphis. His celly was an older Muslim brother from Philadelphia. His name was Khalim. The last brother named Cheese was from Kansas City. They were all good brothers. They gave me a care package to hold me over until my property came. The first thing I wanted to know was who had the yard and hat the cars were made up of? I had to understand my surroundings.

Forrest City was divided between Memphis, Texas, Arkansas, Kansas City, Missouri and Oklahoma City. Those were the biggest cars by state. But then you would have to break up the gang members out of the states. The biggest black gangs on the compound were the GDs, Crips, and Bloods. The Vice Lords had a small car. There were only three Spanish gangs on the yard. Nortangos, Tango Blast, and Mexican Mafia. That made a lot of sense to me because this was not a compound where the Surenos could walk. Given the fact that I just came out of war with them, this is why they sent me here because no matter where I went in the B.O.P. The green light by the Surenos was still on me. I knew that as well, so I was kind of relieved to know I didn't have to worry about them here.

The Muslim community wasn't as big as the Manchester community, but it was still a lot of good brothers here. The Imam was from Philadelphia. His name was Mustafa. Me and him became real tight brothers. We used to work out every morning at 6-7 AM with another brother named Balal. I got a teacher's aide job in the Education Department. It was my job to help guys prepare for the GED test.

Over the six months that I had spent in confinement a new drug was making its way through the Feds; it was a synthetic drug called K2 (aka "Tunchi"). It became so popular because it didn't show up in urine tests. Forrest City was flooded with it. I didn't understand why guys were so strung out on it. The side effects were life threatening. Every day in the unit I would watch guys be rolled out on stretchers or carried out to medical. Dudes were spazzing out, fighting their cellies and everything. The C.O.s didn't really want anything to do with an inmate on K2. I would walk by a guy's cell and he would be lying down in his own vomit on the floor. The word going around in the Feds (inmate.com) was that dudes were dying from using K2. And on top of that I was relearning everything I had forgot about taking the GED.

I kept a positive attitude. In my heart, I knew that God was showing me my purpose. This job would give me the confidence I needed to be a mentor to the youth. I looked at it as a way to stay out of trouble and work on myself. Relearning math, and doing all that reading was just what I needed. There were two more aides that were also assigned to the same class as me. There was Irvin from Texas, and Dee from Arkansas. Irvin was the Number 1 aide because he had been working for Mrs. Booth the longest. Mrs. Booth was our supervisor. But me and Dee were the ones that really ran the classroom. Dee was really smart in math and business. He sharpened me back up with my math. I would learn from him and then teach it to the guys in the class that really wanted to learn. I started everybody out on Algebra. There was no need for basic math. If you were in my class, Pre-GED, that meant you already knew Basic Math.

My first class began at 8-10:00 AM, then we would break for lunch. Then I had the 12-1:00 PM after that. My last class of the day was 1-3:00 PM. Each day before I left, I would set the black board with the next day's math problems. We helped them with other subjects as well. There were really only two subjects that gave everybody trouble, the essay part and math. Teaching the essay was the easy part. All I had to help them understand was how to format the essay. And make sure they stayed on subject. The math was a different story. To be honest with you, because it had been so long since I did any real math I had to brush up on my math skills. Luckily I had Dee to lean on. He was a mathematician. So while I worked the board, Dee would help guys one-on-one. And if I got stuck on a problem, he would help me solve it. We made a perfect team and it showed in the results. At first it was kind of hard to get everybody to participate. But in each class I had a few that wanted to learn. So I focused on them and together we began to make progress. It wasn't long for the rest of the slackers in the class to join in. I think it was because they could see I really cared and was truly trying to help.

Even my boss, Mrs. Booth, started noticing the change. She would give me anything I asked her for. Like if I needed supplies like markers, paper, and pencils. She would run copies for me to hand out homework. I was relearning math and it was all fun to me. I made it fun for my class as well. Guys would want to stand up and work problems out in front of the whole class. I was building up their confidence to pass the test. The trust and relationships I was building with the guys I was teaching got stronger by the day, especially once they knew I really cared, and trusted me to not make fun of them. What they didn't know about me was that I too struggled to get my own GED. I remember back in the state prison, when I was studying to get my GED, there was no student teacher to help me learn. I wish back then that I had an aide like myself. It was only me and the big GED book. I used to take that book into the bathroom and sit in the stall using the light to study because it was dark in the unit and I had to study for the pre-test. Those were the thoughts that motivated me to go hard for these guys.

By the time the first GED testing came around, I had been teaching for 90 days. I felt good about a group of guys out of each of my classes. Mrs. Booth had already given them the pre-GED test and all of them passed. It was one student in my morning class that I knew was going to pass the test with no problem. He was a Spanish dude and he didn't just pass the test, he became the Valedictorian out of all the graduates. Another aide and I earned Teacher Aide of the year since he had come out of our class! Being recognized for my time and work made me feel proud of myself. I could feel God telling me this was my calling in life. This was my purpose; not only to help guys get their GEDs, but to be a leader in helping guys like myself stay out of prison.

After our success in the first GED testing spread around the compound. The size of all my classes grew. Guys realized there was a real chance to get their GED. They started signing up for Education. There were all kinds reasons guys needed to pass the GED test. One of the biggest reasons was because without your GED there was a cap on pay at institutional jobs, no higher than Grade 4. That meant you could be doing the same job as a guy with his GED, but making less money. There was also the fact of you showing the courts your accomplishment of a GED, it looks good when trying to get your time cut. Some guys because of their age were mandated to come to the school area. There was a list of reasons they gave a graduate $25 for passing the test. I had guys offering to buy me food or whatever I needed from commissary out of appreciation for helping them receive their GED. I always declined because I felt like my reward would be from God.

It felt different being respected for doing something good, and not out of fear. Guys were looking up to me for the positive things I was doing in the classrooms. I was shedding the old negative reputation that I carried around with me for so many years. No one called me Miami or Gig, it was either Shahid or Ock! I was more noticed for being a good Muslim brother. The reputation kept me out of trouble. I was sticking to my promise that I made to God while I was in the hole. When I wasn't teaching in class I was spending a lot of time in the law library. I was still fighting my case the best I could. That was a fight that I wasn't ever going to give up on. My faith stayed strong in God.

Forrest City was the Wild Wild West for real. We stayed on lock down because one of the cars was into it over this or that. One week it's the Mexican gangs checking each other in because of control over the yard. Then there was the Memphis car. Most of the time it was over drugs and robberies. It seemed like the Texas car had the same problems. I didn't mind the lock downs. It gave me time to read and write. But I did hate the food. They would bring us these box lunches that were frozen. We would have to hope that the water in the sink got hot enough to defrost them. I learned the best time was early in the morning when no one else was using the water. I know it sounds crazy, but being on lock down to me was a relief from all the stress of everyday prison life.

In my cell, I was able to plan and dream about my future. It was 2015 and I've been down now for 9 years. I was institutionalized in so many ways. The only good part about that was for one, I knew who I was and I accepted it to some extent. It was only natural for me to be a little institutionalized. Look where I've been living for the last 9 years – a correctional institution. The only difference between me and a lot of other guys that were institutionalized (aka "burnt out") was I worked on letting go of the prison mentality. I began to focus on a life outside of these prison walls. Things like the TV or going to the rec yard didn't matter to me. The promise that I made to God and myself while I was in confinement to stay out of trouble would be accomplished by humbling myself; staying out the way. That meant going to the rec yard early in the morning when less people were out. I only went out three days out of the week to get some cardio in. The other days I would work out in the unit.

Me and two other guys used to work out with the buffer machine. I know you may be wondering how you work out with a buffer machine? One thing about doing time in prison, you will learn that some of the most creative people you would ever meet are in prison. Being locked up away from all the luxuries of the world makes you think outside of the box. So we came up with a way to tie ropes around the buffers to hold them together so we could bench press them while lying down on a turned over garbage bin. You would have to see it to understand how we made it work. We also made dumbbells out of sand and cardboard boxes. We had to be careful not to let the officers see us work out like this. Forrest City prison administration had strict rules on inmates working out. They prohibited any upper body working out. This was the first prison I ever did time at that didn't have pull up bars or dip bars for us to work out on. Their reason was not to encourage inmates to become too strong for them to handle. But the funny part about that was inmates didn't have to be too strong to overpower most of the officers there because they were mostly older men and women working there.

There weren't many guys from Miami here. The only real homie I had here was Wayne aka "Fats." He had already been down for 16 years. He was on the same case with the big homie, Kenneth "Booby" William (Black Boy). Fats was part of the south car. It was made up of all the southern states that had small numbers: Georgia, Florida, South and North Carolina. And it may have been a few guys from Alabama. They all sat together in the chow hall. Sometimes when I would wait around to kick it with Fats, I would sit over there too. But everybody knew I was on Muslim time. But just out of respect for the G-code, I gave Fats my paperwork and he gave me his. Fats had pulled himself a local female, so he was getting visits on the regular. And he was doing his thing on the hustle tip. We used to talk a lot about the law. He knew I stayed in the law library working on my case. So he would ask me about different case laws. I did my best to help him, but I always told him to hire a lawyer to represent him. My advice was you hustling anyway, you better off using the money to try and free yourself. It was kind of cool having Fats around to bend a few corners with, talking about the Crib (Miami). We knew a lot of the same people and both had been gone for a long time. So most of the places we talked about were long gone. We would still have stories of the club The Tree in the Sub, and I knew for a fact it was close.

As I was finding peace within myself at Forrest City, the biggest test of my faith in God came in the form of losing my brother Gregg. I remember being called to the Chapel to see the Chaplain. I immediately felt a bad feeling in my gut. The last time I was called to the Chapel it was to be told that my grandma had passed. On my way there I kept praying to Allah that there wasn't anything wrong with my mother or daughter. I never thought about my brother. I guess because he was a man. I had just talked to the whole family a few weeks earlier. The whole family had gathered over my brother's house in Atlanta for Thanksgiving dinner, and even though I don't celebrate holidays I have always been about family unity and get togethers.

When I talked to them all on speaker phone that last time for some reason I got emotional. Not knowing that this would be the last time I would talk to my big brother. I told him how much he meant to me, how he was more than just a big brother to me. He was also a father figure to me. I told him how proud I was to have him as my big brother. My brother was a big joker and loved to make people laugh. Growing up, I was the butt of most of his jokes. So true to comedic nature, he made light of my speech to him asking me what made me all soft and emotional?

Now I was sitting down in the Chaplain's office and he was telling me my brother was dead! I didn't know how to process the news. The Chaplain was talking, but after dropping the bombshell about my brother the only thing I could focus on was keeping myself breathing. From somewhere far off I could hear the Chaplain asking me was I ok, and if I needed to lay down for a few minutes? I couldn't hold my tears back any more. They came slowly. I wasn't used to letting nobody see me cry. So I got up and went to the bathroom to throw some water over my face. When the 10-minute move came, I told the Chaplain I was good, then headed back to the unit.

I was walking in a daze. Guys were speaking to me passing by, and I had no response. I just wanted to get back to my cell. God knew I needed some alone time. My celly was gone on the yard. I closed up my cell and laid down. There was no sleep at first. I did something that I didn't do since my grandma died, I cried myself to sleep. All the memories as kids that me and my brother shared came back to me. I just couldn't understand why? My brother was the good one. I'm the one that couldn't get right. He was the leader of our family. He was the smart one. What would happen to our family? Who was going to help my mom now? I couldn't believe I would never get to talk to my brother again. What about his sons? His wife and who would take care of them now? The more I thought about all the *whys?* the more I felt abandoned by God! But I knew that was not the case. As soon as that thought or feeling came I told myself that God was in control and he knew best.

The news of my brother's death sent me into a deep depression. The next day when I didn't go to work, Dee came by my unit to check on me. He said Ms. Booth was worried about me because it was unlike me to miss a day teaching my class. Once I told him what happened he told me don't worry, he would hold things down. I stayed in my cell for the rest of the week coming out only to shower. I didn't know how to live in a world without my brother. A part of me didn't really want to accept it. I thought if I went to sleep and woke up it would all just be a bad dream. I finally worked up enough nerve to call home.

Talking to my mom made me break down again. I knew I had to pull myself together. If only to be strong for my mom. I was her only child now and she was going to need me to be strong. After our talk, I went back to my cell. I pulled out some paper and began to write because I didn't get to say goodbye. I wrote everything down in a letter. My plan was to send it home so my daughter could read it to him at the funeral. The Feds weren't about to let me go on furlough to go to the funeral. The more I wrote I became at peace with myself. I told myself that the best way to honor my brother was to get my life together. Become the man he would want me to be.

Even as I write this book, his words are still with me. It was his idea for me to write this book. But he wanted me to write about the G-Code. I remember him saying these young guys out here need to know what it is to be a real G and what that code means. There was nobody in this world that knew me better than my brother, not even my mom. He knew I was for real when it came to "Thug Life." The streets were all I knew, and the G-Code was what I lived by. He knew if I told my story it would help inspire some young guys to change their lives.

Losing my brother while I was locked up in the Feds added to the pressure of me really getting serious about changing my life. To me it seemed like God was removing anything or person that I leaned to as my support or rock. I began to understand that God only wanted me to depend on him for everything I needed. I told myself that I would not look towards anyone for help, other than God. Including my mom, I had to learn not to put anybody before God in my life. They buried my brother and with him, a part of me. As the weeks passed into months, so did my depression. I would still have those moments when the thought of him not being here took my breath away. But then there were those times when I was doing something good, like helping one of the guys in my class. I would get that feeling like he was smiling down on me proud of the change I was making in myself. It was times like that when I knew what God's purpose was for me. I understood the reason for all the time I spent in the system. God was turning my mess into my messages. This time in prison was my test. It was on me to make it my testimony. I remember hearing somewhere or reading that, "If you can look it up, then you can get up!" And, yes, the pressure of the Feds had definitely knocked me down on my back. But I never stopped looking up. The time had come for me to move on from Forrest City F.C.I. The last 18 months there had humbled me. I gained more patience and self-control.

My Case Manager called me in to do my progress report. He told me I was eligible for a transfer. My custody level had dropped from medium to low. I wasn't too excited about going to a low custody prison. It meant giving up my cell with a door. Also the lower you go into the Feds, the more likely you are to be around snitches and child molesters. The officers treated you with less respect. I knew I had to readjust my mindset. On the other hand, leaving the medium allowed me the time to work on myself. To focus on my plans for when I got out of prison. In the medium, I had to worry about whether I would have to stab somebody or make sure nobody stabbed me. I gave my case manager the OK for the transfer. Now I had to break the bad news to my class.

I knew a lot of the guys I was helping would take it hard, but would also be happy for me. Ten years in the Feds and I was on my way to a Low. My plan was to spend a year there, then make my way to a Federal Camp. I still had 9 years left on my sentence. My faith was in God, so I was going to miss teaching my class. The feeling I got from helping dudes like myself was uplifting. It gave me a natural high. God was showing me my purpose. He was making me a real leader.

Laundry Man #1

The day came for me to transfer. I was assigned to Yazoo, Mississippi Low. Back in transit, they took me back through Oklahoma. This time I stayed 2 months until they finally shipped me off to Mississippi. It was my first time ever being in that state. On the ride there I couldn't help but to think about slavery. Looking out the window of the bus on both sides of the highway were rows of cotton fields. I could only think about how hard my ancestors had it working in these fields, picking cotton from sun up to sundown. It didn't seem like much had changed in America. As I looked around on the bus, all I could see was young black men in shackles and chains. If our ancestors could endure the harsh treatment of slavery, I knew that I could make it through my time in the Feds.

A lot was going through my mind on the trip to Yazoo Low. I was second-guessing myself. Could I really make it in a Low custody facility? Or was I setting myself up for failure? The level of respect dropped the lower you go in the Feds. Even the C.O.s treat you differently. They talk to you any kind of way. Not only was I giving up my cell, but also now I had to share the restroom with 150 other men. I told myself to trust in God, this was the best move for me. My first day at Yazoo (aka "the Zoo") was a bit to adjust to. It was wide open, kind of like our state prison in Florida. The yard was made up of mostly southern cars. And Florida had the biggest car on the yard. This was the first time in my Fed bid that I was around so many of my homies. I went on the rec yard to meet up with a few of the homies. There was the homie "Madd" from the city, "Geeda" from OverTown, Lil Willie Brother, Dre from Town. Mook from MGT. I made it clear to all the homies, that I was on real nigga time. I told them if you wanted to get closer with me, bring the paperwork so we could swap. I also let them know off top that I was a Muslim. We met on the rec yard after that a few more times, shared war stories and catching each other up on info about the city. Shit like who was getting money, who died, and who was snitching now! After we ran out of shit to talk about. I stopped coming around as much. I had enough of the street talk and who is who. I got a job in laundry on my second day at Yazoo. I never thought I would take a job in laundry. But I have to tell you how God worked this out in my favor.

It's a known fact that when you come to a new prison that laundry is at the top of the must do list. It's the first place they send you after you get off the bus. Well, so happened, when I got to Yazoo they had just fired the whole laundry crew of inmates. It seems that laundry was the mean spot for pushing most of the contraband smuggled through from the camp, and the crew that got fired had run the game to the ground. Since the officers couldn't catch the one that was involved, they fired everybody. It was God's timing for me to be coming right then. The day me and the other guys that came with me on the bus were getting our sizes taken by the laundry C.O. One of the officers asked me, if I knew how to sew and if I wanted a job in laundry? I took the job on the spot. I told myself why not?

At the time I really didn't know anything about working in laundry. I knew there was a hustle in it. But did I really want to be washing niggas' clothes? A big part of me said No! For one, I didn't like interacting with a lot of dudes. Two, my pride was kind of messed up about dealing with niggas nasty ass dirty clothes. I took the job, but I had not really thought it all the way through. That night I laid up in my bed and went over the whys and why nots? Something deep down in me was saying humble yourself, let go of your pride. Trust in God. This job is a blessing.

The next day when I reported to work I had made up my mind to give it a chance. I wasn't the only new worker that got hired. There was Black from Georgia, Steve from Mississippi, Rico from Memphis, Jay from North Carolina. Then they had this one guy from the old crew named Hemphill from Tennessee. We all knew from the gate something wasn't right about Hemphill. How did he get to stay on when the rest of the old crew got fired? The only reason he could be still working is because he was a snitch. He was the straw boss over laundry. The Supervisor over laundry, our real boss, let Hemphill run the place the way he wanted to. In the beginning I didn't care. I followed Hemphill's lead because I really didn't have a clue how to run laundry. So instead of making the snitch my enemy, I kept him close. I was practicing my 2Pac game, keeping my enemy close, taking in everything he told me about the job. Some of the other guys were bumping heads with him. He also gave me the game on how to hustle my wash.

We would divide up the jobs between me and the young boy, Jay. He and I were clerks but I was also the sewer. Rico was the washer. Steve was the dryer. Black was the folder. And, Hemphill was Mr. Laundry: IN THE WAY! I can't lie, working in the laundry was hard work. We would come in at 6:00 am and leave some days as late as 8 pm. Mostly because our supervisor didn't really know how to run a laundry. We were always behind in work.

I didn't mind the work, nor the long hours. It kept me busy and out of the way. I picked up a few clientele from the laundry wash. I wasn't the only laundry man in my unit. Rico, one of the other laundry men, was in my unit. He was a real hustler from Memphis. He sewed up all the wash customers in our unit so I stepped to him with a business proposition. I convinced him that it made more sense for us to partner up. He could handle the wash part and I would fill all the personal orders we got for other things out of laundry. There was always a need for tee shirts, boxers, socks, towels, and blanket sets. Laundry was a prison gold mine. Being a clerk gave me access to all the brand new clothes. I still had to be careful, believe it or not, niggas would hate on you about a prison laundry job, and niggas wanted your job.

I had to watch out for some guys that worked with me, seeing as though we were a new crew. There was a power struggle going on with the crew. All of us were in different cars on the yard. I knew how to play the game without even getting in it. I was going to be patient. And let the haters cutthroat each other out. The dude Steve and Hemphill were at the top of the power struggle. They both were playing the police game telling on whoever they didn't like. I made sure they saw me do as little as possible. There was really no way to keep them all the way out of my business. As time went on things got even better with the laundry job. The first big change came with our supervisors. They were two cool ass white C.O.s from the medium-security prison, Big Mac and Tanner. At first I thought they were going to be hard on us with all kinds of new rules. But it turned out to be the other way around. They did have new rules, but it made the laundry run a lot smoother.

Big Mac had a lot of laundry experience. He and Tanner had run the laundry over at the medium for 15 years. The only reason they left was because of the new Warden. Mac told us that the Warden was making too many changes; he liked things to be left alone. Like he said, "If it ain't broke, why fix it?" I can't lie, I liked Mac and Tanner. And throughout my whole bid, there were not many C.O.s I would say that about. They treated us like men, and gave us respect! As an inmate, that's really all we ask for. They did their job, don't get me wrong. If they caught you stealing or with some contraband, most likely you was going to get written up. Mac might cut you some slack. It all depended on who you were. When Mac took over the laundry, Hemphill lost his pull. Mac didn't like snitches. So this nigga from Mississippi named Steve started putting pressure on Hemphill, and the young nigga Jay from North Carolina. He really called himself trying whoever let him get away with his bullying.

It didn't work on me. I knew he was all mouth. So when he came my way with his wolf tickets, I pulled his card and let him know I was really about that smoke. He wasn't dumb at all! He could tell I was a real one! But the pressure he put on some of the other niggas made some of them quit. After he ran Jay out the job, I became the Number 1 clerk. Mac told me to find a Spanish speaking inmate to work up front with me as the Number 2 clerk. I went out and grabbed one of the little homies from Miami. Castro grew up in the city. He wasn't but 5'2, but had heart. I took him under my wing. I told him to stick with me and he would make some bread. He was a little hard headed at first. Once he saw how much money he could make in laundry, that's when he became Trusty. He got in with the rest of the Trust crew. I was trying to teach him how to move, so he would last long with the job. But once he got mixed in with Rico and Black from Georgia, I had to pull back and let him bump his head a few times. They were stealing everything out of laundry. Mac was starting to notice, and he was getting mad about it because we were running out of stuff that he knew we were supposed to have. I did the ordering so I knew what to take and what not to mess with. So when I would give them niggas the heads up on what not to mess with, they would ignore what I said, and still take whatever they could get their hands on. I didn't care if it wasn't my shit. I just made sure that my name didn't come up when the snitching started happening. It was a lot of back stabbing, throat cutting moves being made. I knew with time, most of them would play themselves out the job. I just had to bide my time and wait. In the meantime, trying to keep my little homie Castro out of the fire. Talking to him wasn't working. He was making them stamps, and that's all that mattered.

Yeah, in the Feds our money was mailing stamps. That's how the cash flows. I set a weekly goal of $250-$300. That gave me a net between $1,000-$1,200 a month. That was the most money I saw working in the Feds. It was better than the Unicor job, by far, with less hours. And this was just the beginning. Once I took over and built myself a real team of guys I could trust, then we could really milk the spot. Castro was the first piece of the team. I hand picked him out of all the Spanish dudes on the pound. He was young and I saw something in him. I made sure his paperwork was good. He was a real nigga. That's why I was trying my best to keep him out the fire with the rest of them thirsty ass niggas that worked in the back. It wasn't long before one by one, they were getting fired for dumb shit.

Black and the fat white boy that folded clothes with him went first. They got hit for not doing their job. Instead all they did was work on the personal wash. Mac came in one day pissed off about whatever and took it out on them. He called me in his office and told me to look around for some new folders. I let the rest of the crew know and asked them to bring me some names. That was my way of trying to include everybody in the process. I kept the final say up to me. I helped this Jamaican brother named Black get the job. So we lost a Black and got a new one. Then Mac hired a white guy named J.R. He was cool. We all knew he got high, but J.R. was a worker for real. We put him on the dryer and he also helped the washer. The good part about him was he wasn't a snitch.

Rico got fired next for washing personal laundry when Mac called for a halt, because the laundry work wasn't getting done on time. We all kept doing our own thing because there was no way for us to put a halt to our personal wash just like that. Rico got snitched on by the nigga Steve. They were beefing about something; I wasn't sure what it was about. Nevertheless, Steve put Mac on to Rico, so Mac gave him the boot. I knew the nigga Steve was playing the sucker game so I stayed out of his way. Sooner or later it backfired on him. I got my Muslim brother Kay-Kay the job fresh off the bus. He was in Manchester with me for years. Kay from D.C., a real laid back dude. I knew he needed the job because he used to work in Unicor with me.

Kay still had a few years left on his sentence. He was always fighting his case just like me. We both were career offenders and been down just about the same time. Kay came in a year after me and had a 30 piece. I got him the job to help him out while he was here at Yazoo. I knew he made a good part of the team. Kay had my back. Steve struck again.

This time it was the young nigga Jay. He ran off. I can't lie, it was really funny how that played out. I was in the front sewing up some pants when I heard the loud fussing coming from the back. I knew it was Steve because he was always into it with somebody. That's when Jay ran in the cage where I was at and grabbed the scissors out the drawer. I didn't see it, but the guys would tell me about it later at lunch. It seemed that Steve wouldn't let Jay put his personal clothes in the wash. So that set it off. Then when Jay tried standing up to him, Steve head butted Jay. Yeah, head butted him! The guys said Jay took off running, so that's what made him get the scissors. It was a standoff for about an hour. I finally talked Jay into giving me the scissors. Then I went into the back and had a talk with Steve. He agreed to put Jay's stuff in the wash at the end.

The next day Jay put in for a job with commissary. Castro finally came around and saw the light after Mac warned him that he was next on the chopping block. So, I looked out again and asked Mac to move him up front with me. I was in need of a replacement for Jay. It made sense because when the bus came each week we always needed a translator for the Spanish inmates. With Jay gone, and no Rico, Steve settled down a bit. He knew that Mac wasn't about to let him keep running guys off, or running to him with the snitching. Besides, there really was no one left to play the rat game with him. Me, Kay and Castro weren't seeing no boo game with the bully shit.

There was J.R., old man Papi, and Jamaican Black. All three of them were so laid back and chill, they just moved around Steve. Everybody was getting money with their personal wash. And under my control and leadership we all were getting a share of the supplies that came off the truck each week. There were all kinds of ways to make money in the laundry. There would be days when the C.O. would go on a unit-by-unit shakedown. They would take all the extra blankets, sheets, and pillows. Almost everything they would take would be sent down to laundry first. And after we went through it, what was left went to the trash out back. Dudes in the unit would send to us, in the laundry, asking us to look for their stuff. They already knew it came with a price. I came up with a rule so things could stay fair and in order. That whatever unit got shook down, the laundry man of that block would have first drops on the loot. With things running so smoothly in the laundry, Mac and Tanner stayed in their office and I ran the show on the floor. With the way I kept things fair with the guys there was no real tension going on. I had Rico working for me in the unit. I would send the personal wash back as early as I could, so by the time I got off work, Rico would have folded and passed out all the bags. He also sold the side merchandise that he or I had orders for. I paid Rico $100 a week on the wash and extra off the merchandise he had sales for. So most weeks he would make up to $200 fucking with me.

Rico was a real hustler. He also sold cigarettes and weed on the side. I would always talk to him about doing too much telling him not to draw heat on what I had going on. I didn't want nobody thinking he was getting cigarettes or weed from me. The laundry was a plug through the camp. And the last crew left it hot, so I had to be careful how I moved. There were other departments that had ways of moving contraband. Food Services, Commissary, Unicor, even landscaping. When one of those departments started busting moves they loved to put out fake lies on Laundry to keep C.O.s off them. But it never worked because when the snitching started, you could always count on them to tell the truth and nothing but the truth. I was cool with the $1,000 I was making a month without no heat. I can't lie, it was tempting to jump in the game. Cell Phones were going for $1,000-$2,000 apiece.

A part of me wanted to get that money off pushing cigarettes, weed, and cellphones. But the intelligence part of me warned me against moving so fast. I haven't been at Yazoo a year yet. There was no way I could already know who I could trust or not. So I stayed in my lane and appreciated the slow but easy money. As each month went by, my account increased by $1,000. I was living as good as the ballers in the prison. My Muslim brother Rashid from Memphis, yeah the same Rashid that was at the Forest City FCI with me, made his way to the Low, a few months after me. We were in the same unit again. So that made us even tighter. We kicked it all day together. When I wasn't at work, we worked out, watched movies, and prayed. Rashid was a fat boy, he loved to eat. He also knew how to cook. We ate good every day. The brother was a bad man when it came to cooking in a microwave. Rashid didn't have to work. He still had dope boy money from the street. He had rental property making money for him. So he never really went to the chow hall to eat. Since I was making money hustling out the laundry, I could afford to eat good right along with him. The one thing I could say about Yazoo Low was there was a lot of money on the compound. It was nothing like Forest City FCI where there wasn't really any. In my unit alone, there was a few millionaire niggas and some big money Spanish dudes.

There was my Jamaican homie Dee, who had his own record label, one of his artists was Papa Doc from Florida. Then there was Big Boss Webb from Queens, New York by way of Atlanta. He owned a few clubs in ATL. One of them was called Room Service. Next door to our unit you had long money Lil B; who was down on the B.M.F case. He was from St. Louis, Missouri, a real nigga with money. There was Block from westside Atlanta. He still had dope money. His homie and celly, Ike from Georgia, also had dope money. Then there was this Columbia kingpin who had major money. There were a lot of money getters of all levels in my unit C-4. It was always a big poker game going on $500 just to buy in. No play money. It was all Cash App, pay up the same day. Niggas would win or lose $1,000 in hours. And, yeah where there is plenty of money there was also just as much drugs. You name it, Yazoo had it. But the number one drug was K2 aka Spice. Everybody was getting money at the Zoo. You had to be disciplined not to get caught in all the illegal activity. The money was there to be made but I always remembered what the OGs used to tell me when I first jumped off the porch.

"All money ain't good money," and "it ain't what you do, it's how you do it!" Last but not   least "In the game, you don't have to be seen to be heard!" Doing time at Yazoo Low was just like being on the block. The female C.O. was on real nigga's jock choosing niggas to put on, or dick and money in return. I had a few offers, but the two C.O. hoes that came at me were out there too hard being dick thirsty for real. And one of them was rumored to have that package. "AIDS!"

I can't lie I was tempted to fuck, but it never happened. I kept working my laundry job and stayed out the way. Those same female C.O.s got walked off for bringing contraband and fucking inmates. They took the niggas to the hole and fired the hoes! I had too much to lose. I had to keep my prison record clean because I knew one day I would get back in court. With my past criminal history, I couldn't afford to have anything new. That was also one of the reasons I didn't jump right into the cellphone game. They were everywhere at Yazoo. And everybody had one, I remember seeing one for the first time. Big Money Webb pulled him out. Bro had it right on him in his boxer shorts. Dudes would have pockets sewn on in the front of the boxers to hide the phone, or stamps, drugs, etc. Webb was showing me on his phone that my Muslim bro CEO Saad and his brother own a club together in ATL called S.L. Lounge. This would be the beginning of me and Webb's friendship or better yet, brotherhood.

CHAPTER FOUR

"Laundry'

The first time I held a cellphone in my hand in the Feds I was scared. It was one of the new touch screen kinds. When I left the streets, it was all about the flip phone like Nextel. These new phones were like computers in your hand. So I was scared I would break it or mess something up, because I didn't know what the hell I was doing. I was also worried about being caught with it. The prison had strict rules on being caught in possession of a cell phone. They were taking good days back, a year loss of visits, a year loss of phone, a year no commissary, and 60 days in the hold. But in my case it could also mean, no play whenever I got my shot back in court. There was a lot to lose from playing around on the phone. But, damn, Webb was showing me Facebook, Instagram and shit was looking good in the world. There was so much I could do on the cellphone. I was fascinated by all I could do. I liked Facetime, the most being able to see who I was talking to in real time. It amazed me, I didn't want to talk the old way any more. I could watch a movie on the phone, even porn. Man this changed the game on how I was about to do the rest of my time. I was still scared and that made Webb laugh at me.

He told me, "Ahk, chill, it's sweet here at the Zoo." Then he finished showing me how to set an Instagram and Facebook page. It's safe to say that I was hooked. Social Media had me.

I still wasn't ready to get my own home yet. Webb was getting them 30-50 at a time. He wanted to put me in the game moving cell phones. Like I said before it was a lot of money to be made pushing cellphones. A new phone could cost you up to $2,000. You could get a used one for $1,000. I really could use the money. But I just couldn't trust all the people Webb had around him. So, I let Webb know that I needed some more time to feel the route out at Laundry. He was cool with that because he already had a good route going through the kitchen. My Muslim brother Rashid got him a phone a week after being at Yazoo. He paid $1,600. He also got a reader and a chip that holds movies and videos on them. The reader went for $200 and the chip cost $50. Rashid didn't care how much all of it cost. All he wanted to do was download movies so he could show them on the unit.

Everybody liked Rashid. He was real easy going. Sometimes I felt like he was a little too easy on dudes. I would have to tell him to fall back off this dude or that dude because they were trying to use him. Webb was the same way, he was a free hearted good dude. I knew that niggas would take your kindness for weakness. I did my best to keep them sucker-free, like I was. Even though I knew I could go to Webb at any time and get me a phone, I didn't, because at the time, I was still getting used to being on a phone. Having a phone came with real responsibility. You had to have a put up spot for when you were out of the unit and they hit with a surprise shakedown. Then there was the part about keeping the phone charged. Because the phone cost so much money you had to be on the lookout for thieves. Yeah, there was big business for cellphones parts. The battery went for $500. You could get like $200 for a front screen. There was even some dudes going around jacking soft niggas for their phones. I wasn't worried about that. Niggas knew who to try and I wasn't one of those. Don't forget about the snitches. They tell on you just to have something to talk about. And with my job, I knew they loved to drop a kite on me so they could put in for my job. So for all those reasons, I took my time before I got all the way in the cell phone game.

In the meantime, I rented phone time. Yeah, niggas were renting out time for a book of stamps ($5.00 a book). You could get 30 minutes for a half a book. We nicknamed it, getting a "Huba!" It was this old school dude from Mississippi named "Spot." He used to rent me phone time. He took his rental service really seriously. Spot would time you right on the minute and be mad if you go over a few minutes. Spot also ran a store. He would buy all the things that he knew guys would want, like potato chips, cakes, cookies, candy bars, etc. So when guys ran out or just didn't make it to the prison store to shop they would go to Spot for whatever. Spot made his money by doubling the price on all his items. Spot was hard to deal with, but he was reliable. I could count on him to have my phone time ready each day, that we had the right C.O. working in our unit.

There were times when a super cop worked the unit when nobody pulled their phones out. Days like that the TV room would be packed. All the game rooms would be full of guys playing cards or chess. But for the most part, my unit (C-4) kept a laid back C.O. on all shifts. The whole 3 years I would stay at Yazoo Low, we had it made. The unit had a lot of cool dudes. I got along with just about everybody, even though I'm not the friendly type. I wasn't a fool. I knew the math, the percentage of hot niggas had to be high in the Low. So I knew most of the niggas that was in my unit was mostly rats! I did what I was trained to do from Day One in the Feds. I made sure I connected with the real niggas in the unit that wanted to be on paperwork time with me. In my unit, there was Block (aka Lucky Lucci on IG), and Yellow Man from Detroit. I had a few homies from Miami there too in the unit with me. Young nigga "Face" from down south. My dog Kevin Johnson from the Scott Projects aka Home Team, Big C from the city. My old school Muslim brother Ginger Bread, Vice Lord O.G. from Chicago. My other old school Muslim brother was North aka David. He was from the city off 22nd Avenue. Ali, my celly from Florida. Can't forget my other celly, Shahid, from South Carolina.

There were a lot of young dudes in my unit. They all had mad respect for me as an O.G. It was nothing to walk by one of their cells, and they were on Live rapping or just talking shit. I wasn't ready for all that yet. I was still getting used to Facetime and really enjoying seeing my family. Block and Yellow were my social media coaches. Yellow was a real smooth talker with the ladies. He would catch me walking by his cell and call me in to show me his latest female on Facebook or one of the dating apps he was on. He had them sending money, taking naked pics. When I walked by and saw his tent up around his bunk, I already knew he was on a freaky date. Talking to Yellow made me feel like my rap game to the ladies was rusty. It had been so long since I even tried to holla at a woman on that tip other than kicking it with a female officer on some PG-13 shit. I knew I still had it in me. So I listened to Yellow and started sending me some friend requests out.

I took pictures and started posting them. I was surprised by the reaction I got. Women I didn't even know were accepting my requests to be friends. I also reconnected with old friends. A lot of them went to school with me. Some I recognized, others knew me, but I was having a hard time remembering them. There were homies reaching out to me that I hadn't seen in years. Because of Facebook I was able to hook back up with homies that were locked away in state prison back in Florida. Me and Bo plugged back in as I did with Frank, my day one brother. Me and Frank had grown up together. He was doing a 30-year sentence for robbery. He had been gone for 20 years now. It was a blessing to hear from him. Bo had a smartphone, so we could Facetime. Every time we did, Bo would have a cell full of niggas on his end. He was putting different niggas on the phone that knew me or knew of me, telling me how they remembered seeing me knock this or that nigga out. I got back in touch with Fred on the Book. My Veli homie Ken and Big Joe sent me a Friend request. He was doing good, getting money flipping houses. The homie B.J. was driving trucks now. Willie Red was fixing houses and flipping them. My homie Curt was driving trucks too. There was so many niggas on the Book with me. It was crazy, so now I had a way to stay up on what everybody was doing. I could see how my family was doing. Who was celebrating a birthday or wedding.

Being on social media made me feel a part of the free world. I could join in on watch parties. Comment on someone's post, make my own post for people to Like or not. Since I wasn't getting much mail or visits

I looked forward to my time on the cellphone. It wouldn't be long before the hour or two I was buying was not enough. My Muslim brothers would let me use their phones. Memphis would let all the brothers ride on his phone. I tried not to take advantage of his kindness. Besides, there were too many of us using one phone. So I went to Webb and told him I was ready for my own phone. On the next drop of cellphones Webb got me one.

I was finally in the game. I got it just in time because I met my future wife Coretta. She was from College Park (Atlanta) living in Texas. I sent her a Friend request and she accepted. So I took a chance and jumped in her DM. With a simple "Hi, my name is Keith. Can we be friends?"

She responded with, "Yeah, holla at me when you get out!"

I told her I most certainly would. But if it was alright I said, "Good morning" and asked her how she was doing from time to time? And just like that we started texting and getting to know one another. I liked her from the very start. She was easy to talk to. Her sense of humor was 100%. We laughed for an hour each day. She worked from home, so she was always home when I called. We would have deep conversations about our lives. I told her I was a Muslim. She wanted to know more about my religion. That drew us closer together. I was lonely and had been praying to God for a good God fearing woman. Asking him for one that would share my faith in Islam. The more I talked with Coretta, I was beginning to feel like she was the one. She asked me if she could come visit me. So I sent her a visiting form.

After all these years without a visit, I was about to have this beautiful black woman come to see me. And it was all because of my cell phone. That weekend she was coming. I stayed up all night on the phone with her. It was a long drive from Texas to Mississippi. We had a good time on the visit. She wore her hair down naturally. I could tell she had a nice body, even though she had on big clothes. She had to wear them because the visiting room officers were big on turning black women around if they wore fitting pants. And you already knew that was hard for most black women to do. Just about all sisters have nice asses. Coretta is really blessed in that area. She has a beautiful smile with perfect white teeth.

When I walked into the visiting room, she ran across the room and threw herself into my arms. If you didn't know better, you would never have guessed that this was our first time seeing each other in person. We hugged for what felt like a long time, but really only for a few minutes. I couldn't help it, so I leaned in for a quick kiss. Our lips met and it felt so natural. I gave the C.O. my ID and we found some sets for the next few hours. I was free on a date with the woman of my prayers. I was so happy to be in visit. I didn't eat any of the snacks she got out of the machine. When it was time for the visit to end, Coretta's eyes started to tear up. I couldn't believe this woman was really crying over me. I could see that she was really sad to leave me behind. My heart was softening for her. This time, I took more control of our kiss, first I kissed both her eyelids kissing the tears away. Then I kissed her soft on her nose, I took my hand and put it on her chin. I gently led her lips to mine. This time our kiss was more passionate. Watching Coretta leave, I told myself that she was a keeper. When I got back to my unit I couldn't hide the smile on my face. All the guys came through my cell wanting to hear details on my visit.

Rashid laid the heavy question on me. Like was she fine in person? Did I get to know her better face to face? I didn't mind Rashid asking so many questions because he was the one I talked to about my personal business. After my visit with Coretta, a lot more of the guys started going harder on Facebook. I would see dudes doing push-ups and then taking their shirt off for pics to put on Facebook or IG. Everybody was trying to get a visit out of some of the women they had hooked up with on social media. Every day somebody was getting caught with a cellphone. It was crazy how dudes were getting knocked off. Like, one guy's baby momma called the prison and told on him for having a cellphone. She waited until he called her then she told them he was on the phone right now. I watched the Lieutenant and two compound officers rush into the unit and go right to buddy's cell. There was nothing he could do.

Our watch out system couldn't save him because all we had set up was a call that we all said when an officer started walking around the unit. That gave everybody time to put up their cell phone. But if you were using your phone in your cell, all you could do was stash it somewhere in your cell. So if they knew you had one, they would search your cell down real good.

In dude's case, they knew in advance that he was on the phone so they knew it was still in the cell. They walked him out with the phone all because he pissed his baby momma off. There were situations where dudes would go Live on social media, and somebody would call in on them. People would send pictures in with dudes in their cell back to the prison. It would be hard for dudes to say that wasn't them. Guys would get in trouble with their girlfriend for all kinds of reasons, for being on social media.

I liked playing around on the phone, watching videos, talking to my girl, and family. But I understood that I had to be disciplined on how I used my cellphone. One of the ways I lost my chance from getting caught on my cellphone was by not pulling my phone out until the 4:00 shift came on. There were fewer officers working after 4:00. And if we had a nasty C.O. working, one I knew liked to catch guys on the phones. It wouldn't come out at all. My girl and family already knew, if they didn't hear from me after 4:00 PM, it wasn't a good night for the phone. Having a cellphone was a luxury everyone couldn't afford. So that led to guys preying on the weak and soft dudes with cell phones. In my unit we had a few of them. There was this guy from Kentucky. He was a cool dude, real friendly. But we all know what being friendly gets you in prison. go. He was cool with me. He would download whatever rap video I asked him to put on my chip. He knew a lot about working the phone. I guess because he hadn't been down that long, and was fresh off the streets. He didn't have any homies in our unit. I don't even think it was that many Kentucky dudes on the compound. Youngster mostly stayed to himself in his cube on the phone, but like I said he was friendly. So guys would always come over to his cube to use his phone. He was so cool, he wouldn't even charge them.

One day I came from work and I could tell right away something wasn't right. I noticed guys in little groups all around the unit. I walked to my cube, so I could get off the camera in the hallway. My celly, Ali was in the cube and so was Rashid. They both put me on what had gone down. It seemed that a nigga from New Orleans had jumped on youngster from Kentucky and took his phone. They said the youngster fought back hard, but he still couldn't get back his phone. He already had let the New Orleans dude use the phone and the dude didn't give it back. So that's how they started fighting. New Orleans had a pretty big car at Yazoo, so nobody wanted to start a war over a phone for a friendly ass young nigga who got played out his phone. I didn't like it because Jit was good people, but I had too much to lose. I wasn't about to play *Captain Save a Nigga*. And besides, shit like that was happening on a daily basis.

The next big blow up in my unit came about because a snitch nigga from Jacksonville, Florida dropped a kite on a C.O. that was bringing in the pack. I'm not going to name the C.O. because they were cool people. It was a female officer, and my homie Jamaican Dee had her on lock. She was cool with me too. When it came to her, she would do her homework on you before she even started talking to you. She was real close to our Case Manager, so she would find out if you told in your case (if you were a rat or not). Because of that she had a lot of haters, mainly the hot niggas didn't like her because she wouldn't fool with them on the hustle tip.

Word on the compound was she had a different nigga on every unit she worked. That wasn't anything new. All female guards that were in the game got down like that. They did their 8 hours or in some cases 16-hour shifts like that. With their prison boyfriend posted up in their office station doorway. My homie Dee had a little more player in him. He didn't do the doorway thing. His girl was a big girl, so she was doing the chasing. All day long she would be sending somebody to get Dee. Yeah, Dee had her bringing him everything from street food, to liquor, weed, and cigarettes. We all knew he was knocking her off every chance he got. Then one of her haters dropped a kite on her and Dee. She told Dee who it was and shit hit the fan from there.

Come to find out, it was nigga I warned Dee about. This same nigga came to our unit because he got caught using a nigga's phone in his old unit. But the fucked up part about it was, according to inmate.com, he snitched on the nigga whose phone he was using. So they let him out the hole and locked the dude up. Then he moved to our unit. When I got the news, I put Dee and a few more bosses up on the situation . I couldn't stamp it because I didn't have any real proof, and the dude he snitched on got transferred. The nigga I'm talking about, we called him Fat Boy, was in on a fraud case. He got in good with a few of the Florida dudes in the unit. That's how he and Dee got in good. Dee would rock with whoever came in the unit from Florida. I didn't get down like that. Everybody already knew I was on paperwork time. I rocked with real niggas from all over. Fat Boy worked his way in on the free phone crew. The "free phone" were Webb's two extra phones. He had a phone for downloading movies and another he let a few of the young guys share. So Fat Boy got in on it until Webb found out about it and put a stop to him using it.

He told the Florida homies, Face and Tee, that he didn't want Fat Boy using the phone because he heard Fat Boy was working fraud on the phone. There was a rumor he was a rat! But what Webb didn't know was that the homie Tee would tell Fat Boy what he said calling him a rat. Knowing that tag caused fights, Fat Boy took it as disrespect. But he didn't address it right then. He knew that Webb was a real boss, and had niggas around him that were ready to go about him. I was one of them niggas, only I didn't follow Webb around all day. I played the cut, but Webb knew I was there whenever he needed me. There was a chain of events that was about to take place that we didn't see coming.

Jamaican Dee would be the puppet master pulling all the strings. Dee was a boss in his own right. He had his own record label. He still had money from the streets. He had niggas working for him. He ran a ticket on the yard betting on all the sports games, and he had niggas selling cigarettes and weed for him. The last thing Dee wanted was to get his own hands dirty. He had too much to lose. Dee had money all over the compound. He couldn't stand to go to the hole and possibly be transferred for jumping on Fat Boy. So he did the next best thing, like a boss. He put some bread on Fat Boy's head. Once word got out that Dee was paying the young wolves in the unit, they knew the money was good. The green light was on. Everybody could feel the vibe. Fat Boy knew it was coming. He was bangered up and waiting in his cell. Three Bloods were the first ones to activate on Dee's orders. They spurred into action.

Two of them were my homies, Lil Rambo and Turow. The other one was Seven from South Carolina. He was one of the 5% Gods. They ran in on Fat Boy and worked him over really quick. Slapped him up pretty bad with the lock in the sock game. There was really nothing he could do but ball up and try to cover his face or take off running. It was hard for him to do anything because of the way they rushed him. He should have never boxed himself in like that. I guess he thought because he had the banger that nobody would try him. That young hit squad wasn't playing no games with him. After they worked him over, they ransacked his cell and took whatever he had of value; his radio, shoes, food, watch, and anything else that could be sold.

While all this was going on, I was in my cell on the phone. Not knowing what was taking place on the other end of the unit. I knew it was tension in the air. I knew it had to do something to do with Fat Boy and Dee. I even knew about the part with the kite being dropped on Dee's girl. But I wouldn't find out everything until after it all played out. My dog - the coolest nigga in the unit, the nigga I gave my Muslim brother, Saad, my word that I would keep my eye on – got hit in the back of his head with Fat Boy's banger. I couldn't believe it. I was so busy trying to hide my cell phone because Dee was beating on the hallway door, trying to get the C.O. to come take Fat Boy out the unit to medical because he was a bloody mess. However, Fat Boy wasn't just going like that.

Instead of getting back at one of the young dudes that beat the shit out of him, this coward "MTF" decided to sneak up behind my dog Webb and hit him with the banger. Webb never had a chance to see him coming because so many people were in the hallway moving by fast, that Fat Boy got right up on him. By the time anybody knew what was happening it was too late. But before Fat Boy could pull back for another swing at Webb, Dee had jumped in and grabbed his arm with the banger. He threw Fat Boy up against the wall and started choking Fat Boy with his elbow pent up under Fat Boy's throat. It all happened so fast, I'm talking about seconds.

Webb getting hit and Dee jumping in to help caused the hallway to be quickly filled with officers all over them. My Muslim brothers Memphis and Gingerbread had already helped Webb back to his cell. They went to work with some wet towels and ice to stop the bleeding on the back of Webb's head. There was nothing I could do but watch everything play out from my cell. I was upset with myself for not seeing the attack on my dog Webb coming beforehand. But there was only so much I could do. Everybody knew that you had to always be on point in prison. Especially when there was tension in the unit. You never knew how shit was going to blow up. That's what happens when you start letting your guard down because you're at a Low-security prison. Dudes are walking around the unit in their shower slides. We call that slipping, getting comfortable. I can't be mad at Webb for getting hit from behind. Then the nigga that done it was gone now. I wanted to break him off so bad because that was a real sucker move he made. Why didn't he get back at one of the niggas that jumped him? He was too scared so he checked in using my dog as a way out.

Once it was all said and done the actions of that night would cause Dee to get transferred. Fat Boy went too. There was no way he could come back to the compound. He was a dead man if he did. After they ran the camera footage from that night, and with the help of their snitches, the SIS team came and rounded up the three Bloods that jumped on Fat Boy. Then a couple of days later they grabbed Webb under investigation. They kept them back there in the hole for about 60 days. Webb stayed for 30 days. We were all glad to see Webb get back out. I hated to see Dee leave like that. He made it at the Zoo. But I knew there was a lot of guys glad he was gone. Because they were in the red with him. And There were those who profited off Dee leaving. Dee had a lot of money left on the compound. His Jamaican homies collected what they could. But I knew they didn't get half of what was out there. Nevertheless, that's how the game goes! It gives and it takes!

I was starting to feel the change at Yazoo. There was still money on the pound, but the yard was flipping and there were more junkies smoking K2 and doing all kinds of other dope. There was a lot more petty stealing going on. I was used to it. I just didn't want it to cause me to turn back to the old me. I knew that I would have to take my chance at going to a camp before I messed it up by getting pulled into the madness around me. The only thing that was keeping me at Yazoo was my hustle. The money I was making was stacking up. By then I was busting a few moves here and there. Whenever my hook up at the camp hit me, we made our move. Everything went smoothly. But in the back of my mind I knew all it took was one slip up, and we all would be busted. It wasn't easy to just quit. We all had too much invested. I was ready to give it all up. I'd come too far to catch a new case, even if the money was good.

Things were getting too close for comfort. The staff was doing a lot of random shake downs because of niggas tripping out on K2. Dudes were getting popped left and right with cell phones. The last straw for me was when we got a new Warden and Captain. They came with this new rule that if you got caught with a cellphone, they were turning your charge over to a special prosecutor. We were facing 1-3 years added to our time. At first we thought they were selling wolf tickets trying to scare us. A nigga wasn't just trying to part ways with their phone that easy. But then this guy named Pimp from Mississippi got jammed up with a phone. A few weeks later after he got out the hole, they told him to pack it up. He was going to the Fed County Jail on a cell phone charge. There it was. No joke. Shit just got real!

The same week they sent Pimp to the county, my Case Manager called me in for my 6-month Team Review. And this time it was good news. I was eligible to be transferred to a camp. My custody points had dropped because I had stayed out of trouble. She asked me where I would like to go to do my camp time. I was caught off guard with this move. I can't lie, I had often daydreamed about being at a Camp. From all the stories I've been told about some Camps in the Feds, it was the closest to freedom you could get while in prison. If your points were low enough, and you qualified, you had to have 10 years or less. You couldn't be in prison for a violent crime or sex offense. There was even a chance I could get a furlough to travel to the Camp on my own. Yeah they would put me on a bus and give me money to eat with. I would have a certain time to get to the Camp. With all this running through my mind, I asked my Case Manager to give me a day to decide where I wanted to go. She told me I could give her three choices, but it all depended on bed space. I already knew what three places I was going to give her; I just didn't know which one I wanted to be my first one.

They were Atlanta, Florida, and Memphis. I heard good things about all three. I couldn't wait to get out of her office to let my family know the good news. But I wouldn't let but a few of my closest homies and brothers know I was about to leave. Damn, this really was happening! God was once again answering my prayers! Now all I had to do was keep trusting and believing in Him. Not only was Yazoo changing, the outside world was too. When I got to the Zoo, Obama was still our President. He was on his last term. I had high hopes on him being in office. There was so much talk about a bill being passed during his time as president. I saw a lot of guys get time off, and the clemency. But I wasn't so lucky. I was labeled a career criminal. To them I was "no Good" and I couldn't get it right. It didn't matter that I'd been down more than 10 years without a write up. Every time they gave out breaks, guys like me got nothing. But all that was about to change, and from the most unlikely source.

It was the end of 2016 and Donald Trump had just upset Hillary Clinton to win the presidential election. I was hoping for Hillary to win because she had campaigned on criminal justice reform to win over the black votes. So when she lost, I took it as another let down. Donald Trump's slogan was "Make America Great Again!" As a Black man in America living inside federal prison making America 'Great' again sounded like taking us back to slavery. Here I was, locked up for 11 years of a 20-year bid, in 2017, far away from Miami in the heart of Yazoo Mississippi. No matter what, I couldn't give up. I was still fighting my sentence, I had a pending motion in court. My chances were looking good. I had already cleared one hurdle.

The courts had granted me the opportunity to argue my career criminal status under this new case "Johnson. Guys were getting out left and right on this new case. I felt like this was my big shot.

CHAPTER FIVE

"First Step Act"

Not only was Yazoo changing, the outside world was too. When I got to the Zoo, Obama was still our President. He was on his last term. I had high hopes on him being in office. There was so much talk about a bill being passed during his time as President. I saw a lot of guys getting time off and clemencies. But I wasn't so lucky. To them, I was "no good" and "can't get right!" It didn't matter that I've been down for more than ten years without a write up. Every time they gave our breaks, guys like me got nothing. But all that was about to change and from the most unlikely source.

It was the end of 2016 and Donald Trump had just upset Hillary Clinton to win the presidential election. I was hoping that Hillary would win. She had campaigned on criminal justice reform, to win over the black votes. So when she lost, I took it as another let down. Donald Trump's campaign slogan was "Make America Great Again!" As a Black man in America, living inside of Federal prison, making America great again sounded like taking us back to slavery. Here it was, 2017, and I was far away from Miami in the heart of Mississippi Yazoo, eleven years into a 20-year Fed bid. No matter what, I couldn't give up. I was still fighting my sentence. I had a pending motion in court. My chances were looking good. I had already cleared one hurdle.

The courts had granted me the opportunity to argue my career criminal status under this new case called" Johnson." Guys were getting out left and right on this new case. I felt like this was my big shot. When you represent yourself, you grow used to waiting on answers from the courts. With the hope of getting my motion granted, and my Case Manager putting me in for the Camp (I had decided on Atlanta), I was falling back and staying out of everybody's way. The last thing I wanted to do was to get into any trouble while I waited on news from the courts. I didn't know which one would come through for me first. My prayers were for the motion to be granted and I went home. But going to the Camp was a little freedom and I would be closer to my daughter.

She was pregnant with my grandson. I was still getting used to thinking of myself as a grandfather. Hope is a funny thing. It has the power to keep you going even when things get hard. During this time there were a lot of rumors that the law was going to change. They had a new bill called the First Step Act. A whole year had passed and I still hadn't heard anything back from the courts. And if that wasn't enough to be called back, Luck, my Case Manager had redone my paperwork for the camp three times over.

Things weren't happening as fast as I would've liked them. I still had my mind made up. The best move would be to leave. The hard part was saying goodbye to the guys like my Muslim brother Ash from South Atlanta. I would sit with him after Juhma service on Friday and brainstorm about business ideas. Bro was already a young black business owner. I knew I could learn a lot from him. It didn't matter that he was younger than me. When it came to getting knowledge, I put my pride to the side. I was also taking advice from Webb. I had asked him how he thought I could get my membership up in my own gym, and he said, "Shahid, that's easy. In Business it ain't always about what you know, but sometimes it's about who you know!"

He told me relationship building is the real key to having a successful business. He said, "I got you. I'll make a few calls and watch, your gym will be filled up with members, paid up for a year."

I believed him too. Webb never talked just to be talking. He always backed up his words with action. I always kept those words in mind. I was already moving like that in my own way. I only really kicked it with dudes that I felt were on making real Boss moves when we touched down in the Free

World. My mindset was always on rebuilding my life. Every day, I spent time on planning my future. Either I was writing or reading a book on ways to start my own business. Being in the Feds, I was meeting dudes from all walks of life. Being a Muslim gave me a brotherhood. I was making life long connections with Muslim brothers from all over the country; Brothers who were getting their lives together. So we could network and support one another once we got out. Oftentimes, after our Jumah Service on Friday you could see brothers in small groups exchanging info or sharing business ideas with each other. One of the brothers who used to give us most of the industry game was former Bad Boy recording artist known as Loon (Mr. "I Need a Girl!" himself). He was no longer Puff Daddy's artist, but our brother known as Amir. When the brother Amir talked, we listened, not just because he was a celebrity.

In the Feds, we are all the same inmates wearing khakis. Amir was very knowledgeable in our religion and had travelled all over the world. So to me it made perfect sense to listen when he was dropping game on whatever he was talking about. And on top of that, he was a real solja when it came to putting in work for the brothers. To anybody that may not know the brother and may presume that just because you heard the song "I Need a Girl" assumed that he's not official, just know that Loon is not the nigga to play with. Let me stamp the real: Loon is a real front line solja ready to go on call. I saw him in action making the call and leading the charge.

When we got into it with the New Orleans car, two of their guys put hands on one of our white Muslim brothers over the TV. It could've gotten bigger than what it did. But Loon and two of the brothers got to the guys before we all did. One of our big brothers knocked out the mean guy from New Orleans, and Loon dropped the other one. Just as I was turning the corner to see what was really going on, it was over. Both of the New Orleans niggas were laid out in front of their unit and everybody was running away. There wasn't anything for me to do but flee the scene myself. Just as fast as it started, it was over with.

Me and Loon were cool. He would come up to my unit and kick it with Rashid and Webb all day downloading movies. We would work out on the weekends together. He was one of the few that knew I was getting ready to leave for a Camp. I still had 5 more years to do. But deep down I felt that wasn't the case. I wasn't about to lose faith. I knew God was going to answer my prayers. I just didn't know how. I had high hopes for my motion to be granted. I just watched my homie from Carol City, Mook, when his name was called for immediate release on the same case I was waiting on.

I was happy for the homie. It's always a good thing when somebody got some play on their case. It gave all of us some hope to wish on. Not long after Mook's good news came, my bad news followed. Another denial was added to the stack of denial letters that I had received over the last 11 years. Whenever I heard my name called at mail call while expecting news from the courts my heart started quaking inside my chest. I knew it was from the courts because I rarely got mail from anybody. So it had to be my legal mail.

I took it hard every time I got a denial. What I hated the most was the judge never gave me a reason why he denied my motion. It hurt because I knew if I had a lawyer my chances of getting out would be better. The only thing about hiring a lawyer was making sure you had something coming in the courts because these lawyers were real money hungry liars who would sell you a dream in a minute. And they loved to overcharge you for a simple motion.

When one door closes it's not over. If you believe and keep your faith, God will open another door. It came during the holidays around the time when a good blessing was needed the most. Even though I didn't celebrate the holiday, I still felt the same homesick blues during the holiday season. A couple days before Christmas (December 18,

2018), Trump signed the First Step Act bill into law. Making the crack cocaine 18-1 retroactive. I couldn't stop smiling when I read the email from FAMM.

Guys were running around the unit sharing the news with whoever would listen to them. It was all over CNN. This was the biggest thing Trump had done since being elected to office. There were other good parts to the bill. It offered good days for programming and working in Unicor, up to 15 days a month. None of the other parts of the bill applied to me. That was ok with me because I was finally going to have my sentence cut. These new changes to the law were a long time coming. I heard guys that have been in the Feds for 20 years saying this was the first time things were really happening for the good. My old head O.G. Muslim brother Ginger Bread from Chicago had been down for 30 years at this time. He had a real shot at getting out on compassionate release this time due to the First Step Act.

There were still stipulations to get relief from the new bill passed into law. In my case, being a Career Offender, I wasn't trying to give the judge no reason to deny me not knowing how long it would take for my case to be called. My mom, Coretta, and my daughter were calling the P.D. office. They were told that I would be given a lawyer, but it would take some time because so many guys benefitted from the law. It was good news to me because I understood how things worked with the system. The fact that they were giving me a lawyer told me that I had this coming. In the past, when new laws came out I felt like it could help me. I would contact the P.D. office and they would tell me right away it didn't apply to my case, mostly because I was a Career Offender. I would never let that stop me from filing a motion on my own.

This time was different. They would do all the work. All I had to do was be patient and stay out of trouble. I decided to make one more big move. The next day when I went to work at Laundry I got the crew together. It was time for me to step down as Number 1. Castro and KK were going to hold it down once I left. I know they were ready and Castro already had a plug at the Camp. Under my leadership we were all getting money. The next move I set in place had all of us looking to make three stacks a piece. I needed every dime I could make. I didn't know what kind of job was waiting for me at the Camp. From what I heard, at some camps they worked you all day and paid little to nothing. A part of me wanted to stay at Yazoo and finish my time up there. I was getting money and I had my phone. Then Webb was looking out, letting my daughter and grandson ride up with his family to visit me. Coretta was coming to see me when she could. That was one of the reasons I was trying to get to the Atlanta Camp. It would make it easy for Coretta and my daughter to come see me. I didn't want to push my luck taking chances on getting caught making moves in Laundry or getting into any other mess on the compound. And there was a lot of shit going on around this time.

One of my homies from Florida named Black put the banger on both of his cellies. He was in a three-man cell with two New Orleans dudes. It all jumped off early one morning when Black woke up to find one of his cellies jacking off while he was sleeping in the cell. Black snapped and grabbed the banger and wet dude up. When he was done with him, he went and found his other celly. He was in the TV room and Black went in and gave him the business as well.

I was at work when I heard the deuces being hit. Looking at the officers running across the compound, I knew something had jumped off, but it could've been somebody freaking out on K2. A minute later, Mac came out of the office with the news. Two guys had been stabbed in the C-1 dorm. I was praying that none of them were my Muslim brother. That was Loon's unit. There were a few brothers down there. I wouldn't have to wonder too long about who or what had happened.

Out came my homie Black surrounded by a group of C.O.s. They had him handcuffed as they walked him across the compound. The medical staff had already taken the two stab victims away. I couldn't tell who they were. But I knew as soon as the yard was back open. I would know the whole story. One thing you could count on in prison was inmate.com. They say that the women talk a lot, but I think niggas talk as much as them, or more! Once I heard what went down, I felt better because Black was in the right. Not even the other homeboys who Black had wet up had nothing bad to say about what Black did. So the situation didn't turn into a war between our two cars. Another close call that I could've been into some mess. Even though Yazoo was a Low, it still was a wild prison. Something was always jumping off.

Waiting on my paperwork to come back to see if I got approved from the Camp was taking longer than I thought. Two months had passed since my case manager had put me in for the camp. I was watching guys that got put in after me, pack out and leave for the Camp. I felt like God was testing my faith. During this time, I was praying more and fasting. My relationship with Coretta was growing. She was learning more about Islam. That made me feel like she was the one for me. It felt good to have her on my team. I would spend hours on the phone with her, making plans. When I wasn't on the phone I began writing. The idea for writing my life story came from my little brother Jay.

I remember him saying, "Bro, you need to tell your story. These young guys need to hear what a real G thinks and how he moves."

At first I thought writing a book wouldn't matter to anybody. Then I had a change of heart after seeing how many young guys came to me for advice. They looked up to me as an O.G. that had "Game" to "Offer" them. In doing so, I was also helping myself. Doing time in prison gave me an opportunity to reflect over my life. I had some work to do if I wanted to break this cycle I was caught up in. I was praying and asking God to help me make sense out of all the time I had spent in prison. With that in mind, I felt like he was telling me to write the change I was seeing in myself. I began to like the idea. I felt more disciplined over myself.

It's been over 10 years since I smoked a joint of weed or drank any kind of liquor. I was doing better with my temper, not getting into any fights. The respect I used to get from fighting, now came from being humble. I wasn't the only one noticing my change. The homies that knew me from back in the day would comment on how laid back I was now. Every day I told myself that God gave me these 24 hours. And just because I was in prison, I wouldn't let that stop me from working on becoming a better me. I remember a conversation with one of my counselors back when I was in juvenile. He was giving me some advice on life

He broke it down in terms of a football game. "Like a football game with four quarters" – Life could be looked at the same way. In the game of football, you could be losing in the first or second quarter, then there was halftime. That's when you take a look at what you are doing wrong in order to stop losing. Or, on the flip side, you could review what was working for you. Then you could come back out of the locker room with a new game plan. His point to me was to use my time in juvenile as a locker room, and keep my faith because the game is won in the 3rd and 4th quarter of the game. Sad to say, I didn't take heed to his good advice then. But I never forgot his wise words.

It was thoughts like that good advice I got all those years ago that were coming back to me because I was writing. I realized that I should write a book that people in prison could act upon. I thought people in prison or in jail could learn from my decisions made during my imprisonment. Something inside me was telling me to share my journey. I had doubts in myself about writing a book. It wasn't easy to start. I prayed to God to give me the courage to believe in myself. Also the wisdom and knowledge to complete my goal. All I had was a GED that I got in state prison years ago. I was self-educated. I always had a problem with my spelling, but I didn't let that stop me. I armed myself with a dictionary and told myself that God would help me. Besides, it was Him that gave me this message.

I really believed writing this book and telling my story would help me change my life and help some young guys coming through this system have hope. Because if I could change and turn my life around, then anybody that truly wanted to could. I remember reading in the Quran that Moses couldn't read or write, and had a speech problem. But God still chose him to deliver his message to the people. I knew I wasn't Moses, but I do serve the same God. There were also men like Malcom X that did time in prison and was self-educated. If I found confidence in examples of those great men of God, it was my hope that young men would read my story and be inspired to change their lives. Breaking my time up each day between working at Laundry, working out and writing, helped me stay out of the TV room, cards and game room. I stopped going to the rec yard. I was never into prison sports. And Yazoo didn't have a weight pile, so I just worked out in the unit. We had a pull up bar in the shower area. Days turned into weeks and weeks into months.

I was still waiting for the news of if I could go to the Camp. Then just like that, I was getting off from work when I walked into the unit, my Muslim brother Rashid informed me that the secretary was looking for me. I hurried off to her office. I couldn't help but smile to myself. I knew it couldn't be but some good news.

I knocked on her door. She was expecting me. Before she even said anything, I could tell it was good news. She was smiling when she said pack your stuff you will be leaving on Monday to the Camp in Atlanta. I thanked her, then walked out of her office in a daze. It was finally happening, some freedom. No, I wasn't getting out, but I still felt like I was. I couldn't wait to tell my family. As I walked back to my cell, I allowed the news to sink in. I was really about to go to a Camp, not any

Camp, but the one in ATL. The feeling I was having was surreal. I was hoping for a furlough there. That's when they give you a bus ticket and tell you to get there by a certain time. But that wouldn't be the case. When she gave me the good news, she also told me that I would be leaving on the prison bus with 17 other guys that following Monday. It was cool with me as long as I was going!

Rashid was still waiting for me in my cell when I got back. There was no hiding my good news from him. He could read me like a book. We hung out all day. We worked out, ate, prayed and kicked it every day. I was going to miss my Muslim brother. Doing time, for as many years as I had, you get used to saying goodbye. It was just like that. Everybody had their own date. Some were longer than others and some were shorter. Rashid didn't have that much more to go.. At the time I had more years to do than him. Rashid couldn't go to the Camp. He had too many phone write ups. Nevertheless, he was happy for me and he told me as much. After letting a few of my close friends and brothers know my good news, I asked Rashid to use his cell phone. I had already sold mines for a stack. I called my mother then my daughter. I saved Coretta for last because I knew she would want to talk the longest.

The word spread fast through the unit. Guys were stopping by to wish me luck and see what I didn't want to take with me. Because I was expecting to leave for some time now. I was really prepared. Everything I wasn't taking with me was already promised to who would get it. I made sure the guys I wanted to exchange contact info with had mines. It was much easier now with social media. Everybody had a Facebook or IG page set up. So that's how we stayed in touch. The 3 years I had been at Yazoo, I grew close to some real guys. But my time there had come to its end. I knew enough about life to know that I may never see some of them again. But there were those that I would later on in life.

I still had the weekend to say goodbye. So I gave Rashid enough food to cook a good meal for us over the weekend. The rest of that day, I began to pack the things I would take with me. Later that night I laid in my cell looking up at the ceiling contemplating the many bad decisions I've made during this time. But now I felt things were turning around for me. I was starting to see a light at the end of the tunnel. I was looking forward to Camp life.

CHAPTER SIX

"Camp Life"

My time in prison made me a light sleeper. So when the C.O. came into my cell with his flashlight. I was already awake. Before he could touch my leg to wake me, I sat up. He asked was I inmate Hunter #31595-074.

I said, "Yes."

He told me to roll it up. I was leaving. They needed me in R&D by 4:00 AM. When he left I rolled over to look at my alarm clock. It was 3:00 AM, that gave me an hour to be ready. Both of my cellies were still asleep. My Muslim brother Ali slept on the top bunk and Small Face from Memphis was our other celly. He was a fifty-year-old gangbanger (G.D.). He worked in the kitchen and stole everything he could get his hands on. He hustled his ass off just to give it all to the dope man. Nevertheless, I got along with both of them. Now that I was leaving them, I had already broken off everybody what personal property I wasn't taking with me. It was Monday morning, and I had all weekend to say my goodbyes. I woke Ali up and told him I was out. He got up to help me with my bags. I still had like half an hour left so I took a quick shower. Then I went to Rashid's cell and told him I was gone. Everybody else would have to find out when they woke up. Besides, all of them knew I was leaving Monday anyway.

I wasn't the only one leaving out my unit. There was one of my homies from Florida named "Spot." He was an old school "G." He had been down for 17 years and was finally on his way to the Camp. Then these two Spanish boys were also going with us. Once we got to R&D (Receiving and Discharge) to pack out our personal property. That's when I noticed it was 20 of us going to Atlanta Camp. I was happy to see my Muslim brother "Tone" from East Detroit. There were a few more guys I knew from around the compound, Big C from Florida. Jay from South Carolina. I really didn't know the rest of the dudes other than seeing them come through Laundry. Because there were so many of us going to the same Camp, the prison decided to put us all on a bus and take us directly to Atlanta. In one way I was disappointed because I was hoping for a furlough to the Camp. On the other hand, I was glad we didn't have to go through transit. They would've sent us all the way to OKS to lay over from months just to go back down south to Atlanta. Sitting in the holding tank in R&D listening to a few other guys talk, it seemed that a few of them were already told they were getting a furlough pass to go to the Camp only to be told it wasn't going to happen now. And this was how they were getting to Atlanta. They were pissed off because they had already set up arrangements with their girls who had booked hotel rooms and rental cars.

One of the Spanish boys had a plane ticket booked. One thing I learned about the BOP is you can count on them to change up on you at any given time. Them being upset didn't last long before you know it we all were talking about how good we heard the Atlanta Camp was. The Word through inmate.com was it used to be super good time until some dumb ass went Live on Instagram and somebody sent it to the local news. The Warden was so mad he backed the bus up and transferred just about everybody at the camp and put the camp on lockdown. It used to be 500 inmates, now from what I heard, it was under 100 down there. I wasn't too worried about all the restrictions they said were going on at the camp because I wasn't planning on being there that long.

I was still waiting on my good news coming from the courts on the First Step Act crack law. Dudes were already getting out on it. So all the stuff these guys talk about with regards to all the rules and not being able to do this or that. I didn't care, as long as I got to visit with my daughter and grandson also to see Coretta. I was good. They could have all the smoking and drinking and partying all they want. I'm thinking about going home. I could see the light at the end of the tunnel now.

From Yazoo, Mississippi to Atlanta, Georgia was a five-hour drive. I slept for the first 2 hours. It was still dark out. When I woke, the sun was just peeking out above the horizon. We still had three hours to go, so I took in the free world view from the bus window. It had been so long since I saw the city lights and cars in traffic. It was hard getting comfortable on the ride because we were chained up with our hands cuffed in front of us. The bus was really cold. I took the bag that our lunch came in and stuffed the air vent next to my seat. Lunch was a pack of bread and two slices of bologna with crackers. I ate the crackers and used the pack of bread for a pillow. It was mostly quiet on the ride. That gave me time to think. Preparing my mind for what was ahead of me. I knew it would be a lot of disrespect, according to the way I was living in prison. Because in the Feds the lower you go in prison the type of guys you are around change.

At the Camp, there were dudes that had never been to prison. They self-surrendered straight to the Camp. So I would have to expect them to be all over the place, in the way. I told myself it's up to me to create my own lane to move in. I didn't at the Low in Yazoo, and I will do it at this Camp. Smiling to myself, things were finally looking up for me.

Pulling up at Atlanta Federal Prison, it reminded me of all the old prison movies. The prison seemed out of place sitting in the middle of the city surrounded by old wooden houses. The first thing you noticed about it is, this big ass concrete wall that goes around the entire prison. It was one of the oldest prisons in the BOP. It was built in the 1900s and was over 100 years old and even Al Capone had served his Fed sentence here. We pulled into the west gate garage and waited until the door closed and the officers put up their guns. Then they unlocked our cuffs and we all got off.

They checked us in, gave us yellow jumpers to put on. After that, they called down to the Camp. In about 20 minutes they were releasing us. The town driver was an older guy. I would soon find out it was my home boy's dad from Overtown in Miami. He was cool, but in time I would see that he was burnt out ("institutionalized"). He had to make three trips to take all of us to the Camp. From the west gate to the Camp was about a good mile walk. It was a walk that I would end up getting used to because my job would be right next door to the west gate.

Standing outside the prison without a gate or officers with me felt strange. But I was enjoying it and taking it all in little by little. The gate to the Camp was open. Me and the second group of guys dropped off by the town driver made our way through the gate. Our first stop was the Officer in Charge ("OIC"). There was only one officer working at the Camp. She gave us our cell assignments. I was assigned to a cell with an old white man named P.D. He was really laid back. We exchanged names. I let him know I was real and he could see my paperwork as soon as my property arrived. He told me he was in for a meth charge and that he had been at the Camp of 5 years. I wouldn't be P.D. 's celly for too long. Come to find out he snored like a bear. I left in a week.

My new celly was from Chicago. His name was Heavy. Yeah, it fit him because he was every bit of 350 pounds. Real fat boy. He talked a lot and I really believed he put on a 10 on every story he told. Heavy had every car in the game. He hustled and owned all kinds of businesses. When my property came, I pulled out my paperwork and laid it on his bed for him to read. He didn't return the act, so I can't say if he was real or not. I was relearning myself on how I bid at the Camp. I would focus on my goals, getting ready to return to society. I only cared about building relationships with guys I could network with. Since I wasn't hustling, I used this time on writing books and working out. I was still waiting on news from the court. I also read books on business, finance, and preparing myself for success. The more I could learn about business, the better prepared I would be for the challenges upon my release. Camp life was really laid back. It gave me the time I needed to create a plan. So I started strategizing on how to better use my time while I was at the camp. I got the job I wanted working in the staff gym.

The job consisted of cleaning up the restrooms and putting the weights up after the guards. But I got to work out myself. So it was a good job to me. I went to work at 6:30 AM – 10:00 AM. Then I came back to the camp. Shower, then write for two hours a day. Afterward, I would read and take a nap. In the evening, I would sit outside because the weather was good in Atlanta. Some days I would play a few games of chess and take walks around the track. Those walks I would have a talk with myself, asking myself questions, trying to understand what I wanted out of my life. I knew I was tired of this cycle of going in and out of being locked up. I could see the change in myself. I was 12 and a half years in the Fed bid. I've given up smoking and drinking. Nor have I had any write ups for fighting or anything else.

I know that I have been blessed. God was showing me favor. But to my credit I was showing God my gratefulness by staying true to my promise to Him. That I will practice Islam and keep my faith in Him. The Camp was just a new test of my faith. There was anything and everything to do at the Camp. When me and the guys that came with me to the Camp, there were only 90 inmates total. When my group got there we took the count to 110 inmates. That was still a very low number compared to how many inmates the Atlanta Camp is used to holding. It seemed like the staff over the Camp was screening who they were letting come to the Camp now. After I talked to a few of the guys that were left from the last group of inmates. I had a better understanding of how wild it was before I got there. It made sense to me to listen to everything these guys were telling me.

There was Flossy from Georgia. Tank from South Carolina. Kevee from Florida. Mac G from Tennessee. Dee was from North Carolina. I knew him from Yazoo. Then there was my homie Skibo from Florida. He worked in landscape. It's a good job because you had the run of the whole compound. The landscape had the best opportunity to get all the contraband in. I needed a phone. Just about everybody had one, unlike the Low at Yazoo. Cell phones were really cheap. The word was they were going for $150. But since we came and the demand for phones was up. So the guys that had them for sale jumped the price up to $300. That was still better than $1,600 - $2,000. At the Low, the nigga Flossy and Kevee had the market sewn up. The Spanish boys were on some playa shit. They were doing it the right way. Every new Spanish dude got a free phone and they smoked, drank, and ate together. Basically they took good care of each other. Like always, niggas did the opposite and tried to hustle each other. I didn't jump right into the game, I was still watching and studying everybody. Even the officers paying attention to everything. I wasn't trying to be a part of the static of inmates that got knocked off for contraband and sent back to the Low. One of the first niggas step up on some real nigga time with me was Tank from South Carolina. He let me get 2 hours a day on his cellphone. Using his cellphone helped me set up my first move at the Camp. I had a few homies that lived in Atlanta and a couple Muslim brothers also. I reached out to my Muslim brother Ash from the South Side. I told him what I needed. He told me, whatever it was, got me.

I got with one of the Camp runners. Those were the guys that were making moves by cutting the gate so they could meet up with their connect on the outside. For their services they charged according to what the package was. I made a deal with Flossy. I would have my homie Block drop my phone off to one of Flossy's spots. Then I had my Muslim brother Saad send him $50 Cash App. When I got my new cellphone I was back in contact with my guys I left at the Low. I made myself a schedule for using the phone. I would stick to the same routine I had at the Low. I only used the phone after the 4:00 PM count. The chance of being caught was less because there was only one officer that worked during that time.

There were guys that hung out on the phone all day long. They had no regard for the staff. It wasn't just being on the phone, dudes would be walking around drinking and smoking being loud for no reason at all. To them every day was a party. One of the main guys that partied the most lived in the cell right next to me. Dee was from North Carolina. He was cool and loved to sing when he was drunk. And that was all the time. Dee was at Yazoo Low with me. But he had been to the Camp a year before I got there. He would leave the Camp in the morning at 8:00 AM and meet up with his girl. She dropped him back off around 2:00 PM.

Dee couldn't wait to shove his stank ass finger in my face. "Yeah, nigga, smell that! Bet you don't know what that is?" He would ask me with his big ass smile. I know exactly what the smell was, pussy. I don't care how long I've been gone; the smell of sex will never be forgotten. He would give me full detail of his day at the hotel. I wanted to go so bad, but I was scared I'd get caught. And Coretta wasn't havin it. She would tell me don't even think about it. We have too much to lose and besides, what would happen if we got caught. How would we explain what happened to my mom? I was not trying to have an escape charge on my jacket. So the judge could see that. Dee would make it seem so easy. He had it down pat. He would take his phone with him. So that if anything happened back at the prison like an emergency count and he needed to be back very quickly, one of the guys would call and let him know about it. The hotel wasn't but ten minutes away. He always had a change of clothes with him so he could take the yellow jumper off. I knew it wasn't going to last long with Dee because he was too loud with it. And he stayed drunk all day. Even when he was leaving, he had beers and liquor stashed all around the Camp. I remember the day it all came down for him.

It was a little after 3:00 PM on a Friday. I was laying in my bunk when I heard this woman scream, "Stop it! Give that here!" Then it was more loud yelling. I didn't even get up to see what was happening. I never run into a situation that didn't have anything to do with me. I wasn't trying to be nobody's witness. I laid there and listened. I knew all the voices. It was our day shift officer. She was going off on Dee. She had already called back up to help. And when they showed up, she got even more worked up. They had Dee handcuffed and was all up in his face talking shit. Come to find out later that she saw Dee with a bottle of liquor. She talked him into giving it to her, making him think she wasn't going to write him up. But that was a lie, and when he saw it,he grabbed the bottle back and took off on her.

He ran around the unit and turned the bottle up, drunk as much as he could then threw the bottle away. She was pissed with him. The guys that went to see what happened told me she was hitting him in the face while he was handcuffed. That was the end of Dee's Camp life. My next door neighbor was gone back behind the fence. He had his way for a long time.

Incidents like what happened with Dee was normal. To me it was like watching a funny prison reality show. There were so many dudes getting caught with contraband and in some cases it was their own stupidity that got them knocked off. Other cases were due to someone snitching. That wasn't no surprise to me, we were in the Feds and that's what type of guys that are mostly in the camp. For the most part, staff didn't need a rat to tell them where the contraband was. These dumb ass dudes would put stuff in the same spot every time. It was too easy. Even the C.O. made fun of how stupid niggas was. They would make jokes like, "Because of the camp, they don't ever have to buy cigarettes or liquor any more." I could never understand the shit these dumb ass niggas used to do. It was like they were hustling backwards.

For example, a pack of cigarettes went for $20-$25. Out of 150 inmates at the camp, only about 50 smoked. Break them 50 smokers down to a pack a week, that's all the cigarettes you needed to buy weekly. So why would you bring in 300-400 packs of cigarettes at one time? So now you have to stockpile the packs. Taking the unnecessary risk of the packs being knocked off. So you end up losing money. It just didn't add up to me. I did the math, counting the fact that there were too many guys competing for the same market. From the outside looking in, I could see all the cutthroat antics, and backbiting going on among the dudes that were hustling. To my calculation it couldn't be no more $1,500-$2,000 circulating in the camp economy. It wasn't enough for me to take the risk. After you divided the money up with the other guys that were hustling, you were good to make $100-$200 for your trouble. Most of the guys hustling were just supporting their own habit. Every month wasn't the same. Some months you couldn't even count on the $1,500-$2,000 because the demand for cell phones would be down. Everybody had one. If there were a lot of cigarettes on the pound. Nobody would be buying them.

During one of these periods when the money was flowing, two of the hustlers started spreading a rumor of a big shakedown coming. And that the staff was going to run background checks on any phone finds. They convinced me and a lot of other guys that it was best to break up our phones. I didn't want to at first, but the more I thought about it, it made sense not to chance it. So just like that I took my phone outside and broke it to pieces. I went without a phone for a month. The shakedown never happened. But the hustlers got what they wanted. They sold out of cellphones. I charged my first phone to the game. Yeah, I fell for their trick.

My money was real tight, I put myself on a one-year budget. My hope was the judge would rule on my motion. From all the cases I've studied with the same issue as me. Everybody with just as much time as I had was receiving immediate release. In fact, two guys there with me got immediate release. One was from Florida. His name was Skibo. The news would come back to us a year later that some young dude shot and killed Skibo over a woman! The other guy was Big Mike from Georgia. He didn't even know that a lawyer was working his case. He was surprised when they told him to pick it up. He was getting out. Watching them leave and hearing about guys getting out from behind the wall on almost a daily basis gave me the hope and faith I needed to stay focused on preparing myself for my day. I knew it was coming.

I ended up getting a new phone. This time my little bro Jay came through for me. My dog in the Atl, Block, dropped this one off too. Block was a real partner I could count on. By this time, I was more comfortable on how to move at the Camp. Everything was smooth. I had the job I wanted. I was getting visits, bonding with my daughter and grandson. The year went by fast. 2019 was on the way out. The new millennium was here. My lawyer had contacted me twice informing me that things were looking good in my case and that the judge would be making a ruling soon in about 90 days.

The new year came in with death instead of life. This was supposed to be the year of vision at least that was the motto of everybody posted on social media: 2020 vision! I saw one post that made me really think it said "The 1900 was gone, so our teenage years are over. Now it is 2020, it's time to grow up!" Everybody was claiming this to be their year to start a business, save more money, or invest more. We were all excited for the new year to come in. It was the year of change and people wanted Donald Trump out of office.

America was split in half by race. It was an election year for the presidency. As far as I was concerned politics was a money game. The voting part was all for show, they put that process up to make the little guys feel a part of the game. Like he had a voice at the real table. Don't get me wrong, I know the importance of voting due to the respect of our ancestors fighting and laying down their life for the right to vote. So I would never speak bad about that right being taken away from me made me look at the whole process from a different standpoint. I studied the teachings of one of our greatest black leaders of the past, Marcus Garvey and his message was to us Black people to get our money. Build our own businesses, buy our own land, control our own economics, and control our black dollar. See, to me, it was clear: Money, Power, Respect!

You gain control of your money, that gives you power, with the power comes respect. But what was wrong with my people today was the same thing that was wrong with them in the past. It began with our fake ass leadership. The ones that sold out their soul for spots at the service table in the back of the White House! They keep pushing the same weak submission, begging the white man for equal rights at his table by voting and marching. Instead of educating the people of economic power for themselves. They were too scared of doing that because then their white master wouldn't need them any more. I wasn't worried for my people because I was woke. And God had blessed me with time to study and gain understanding. I knew that this system of racism would not win, it would not destroy us. We as a people have been through the worst. I think about our ancestors on them boats making that long horrible trip from Africa and the sacrifices that were made. How strong they had to be under those conditions, but they lived, and pressed on so we could live today. Knowing that gave me hope. We're made up of their DNA. In my studies, I have learned a pattern of God. When it came to people being oppressed by power in authority he would always turn the oppressor's plan around. What they meant for evil, God would use for good and raise a consciousness of love and unity among the people.

The death of Nipsey Hussle was a powerful spark of light. His life with the message in his music of entrepreneurship, buying back the hood was registering with the people through his Marathon Continues movement. It was sad to lose a great mind like Nipsey. After listening to his music and learning more about the young brother. That he was the kind of young rapper, that real street niggas needed as an example. His influence was strong among the gangbangers. Being a known Crip and repping his blue flag because that was his set in California, Nipsey had real love for his hood and invested back by opening his clothing store and shopping center called The Marathon. The love and respect Nipsey received in his death transcended into peace between Bloods and Crips all over the country. The impact was felt in the Feds prison as well. I knew for a fact that gang members were forming a coalition built on paperwork in response to the growing number of Mexican gangs. The consciousness of black unity was growing in the streets and penetrating prisons.

L.A. became the center of our pain and love with another impactful death. I walked in the TV room to use the microwave. I looked over at the news and saw Breaking News on CNN that legendary basketball player Kobe Bryant and his daughter GiGi were killed in a helicopter crash. When the official news report came over the TV screen, it was like my eyes were seeing the news, but I couldn't process the information. This couldn't be true. Kobe was so young. And his daughter was a little girl. Altogether it was reported that 11 people had lost their lives. The only way I could describe myself and most of the guys that was locked up with me on how we took Kobe's death was a total shock. We couldn't understand how Kobe could be dead. All of us were big sports fans. To us, Kobe was too big to die like that. The sudden way Kobe died, had everybody taking life more seriously.

One of the posts that everybody was reposting online read: "Leaving your home and returning was a blessing!" Overnight all of Kobe merchandise sold out. Everybody was trying to get a piece of legendary life. Tributes in honor of Kobe and his daughter went up all over the country. Celebrities and athletes were all over TV paying their respect. The Laker organization allowed fans to set up a memorial out in front of the Staple Center. It was a sad time for sports fans and everybody in general. The new year was just getting started.

2020 was just getting warmed up with the loss of Kobe and his daughter. It wasn't that far after watching the televised memorial service for Kobe and his daughter when suddenly the headline changed to worldwide news of a new virus called COVID-19. It was first detected in a fishing city in China. The virus was considered to be a strong, deathly strain of the flu and highly contagious. It could be transmitted through the air or any means of physical touching. The spread was rapid. What had started in China had turned into a worldwide pandemic virus outbreak. It was like nothing I had ever seen in my 45 years alive. People were dying by the 100s every day. The whole country was on lockdown, being quarantined under mandatory stay at home orders that were being enforced. Businesses, schools, even the courts were closed. The world was getting a taste of being confined. For those of us that were already incarcerated, things got a little tighter. It got worse for inmates in the pen and medium prisons, as they were kept behind doors on lockdown.

I was happy to be at the camp. My chances for an early release were better. And we couldn't really be put on a real lockdown. Our cells didn't have doors. And even our units never were on lock. We could go in and out as we pleased. But what they did stop was our visits, and for a few weeks they weren't letting us go outside the gate to go to work. We weren't allowed to eat together in the chow hall anymore which didn't make any sense at all to me. Because we would still line up, not 6-feet apart as suggested by the CDC. We would get our trays and still go back to the unit and eat together anyway. Social distancing was impossible. That's why so many other countries were releasing their non-violent, and offenders with medical conditions, but not in the Good old land of the Free ("America"). This country was dragging its feet when it came to the wellbeing of their incarcerated population made up mostly of black and brown people. While they were taking their sweet time, the virus was claiming lives in the prison system. The state and local prisons took action first. Leaving the Federal prison looking stupid and racist. Under pressure, the Attorney General Barr directed the BOP to review all inmates for release under a bill passed by Congress called the CARES Act. It gave priority to inmates 65 and older, or those with preexisting medical conditions. Then if you had 18 months or less with no violent charges. There was a whole list of things that kept an inmate from getting out early. I didn't get my hopes up high on getting released on the CARES Act. I was still waiting for my motion to be answered. That would be my way out.

Three months into 2020, and the pandemic had people in their homes, there were memes going up online making fun of people. One I really enjoyed seeing said, 'Now y'all know how we feel in prison!' Another said, 'If you crying about being locked in your house, stay away from me because you will tell something!' The only people that were allowed out were those whose jobs were considered essential. It was a mandate to wear a facemask when you were out in public. We were experiencing the same rules at the camp. The BOP enforced mask wearing and restrictions throughout all Federal prisons. Watching CNN, I was able to keep up on the spread of the virus. It was the first time I ever saw a body count on national TV. It showed the global total cases and total cases in the United States with the death count. It was crazy looking at that death number growing every day. Each number represented a life gone. Updates were coming in by email from FAMM, an organization that advocated on behalf of federal inmates.

The first death in the Feds came from a Low in Louisiana, Oakdale Low, a 46-year-old black inmate. The first death of a staff member was right here in Atlanta, behind the wall in the Fed pen. The staff was a black female Case Manager. She was in her early 30s and took us all by surprise. Up until the death of the young Case Manager, Atlanta Fed prison was dragging on releasing inmates under the CARES Act! Because the BOP was on a lockdown. They stopped all transfers between all Fed prisons. At the camp, where I was, the staff opened up one of the units that was closed. Our counselor asked anybody in a 2-man cell if they wanted to move to the new open unit. That gave everybody a single cell. Guys were leaving left and right. We went from having 150 inmates down to 80 inmates. A few guys tested positive for the Coronavirus.

When word spread about the positive tests, we all became worried. I admit I was scared. I became obsessed with washing my hands. I kept my facemask on whenever I left my cell. My fear was dying in prison after doing all this time. All I could do was pray and hope that I would stay healthy. I could tell other guys were feeling the pressure. When I turned to praying, other guys turned to drinking every night. The first wave of inmates released under the CARES Act were all white. This caused a lot of racial tension. The black and Spanish inmates were feeling like our Case Manager was overlooking our cases. I wasn't getting caught up in that fight with the staff. Over my time in prison, I understood that the staff was going to stick together. A lot of the black inmates started writing the case Manager up, accusing her of not doing her job.

She was a senior officer with over 20 years working for the BOP. So I knew better than to make an enemy out of her. She knew all the tricks on holding up your paperwork for release. She was the only case Manager for the whole Camp of over 100 inmates. Her way of playing the game started with her taking an early vacation right at the beginning of the pandemic when a list of 30-40 guys names came down for review under the CARES Act. This move sent most of the guys into a panicked rage. Not me. I kept my faith, and I encouraged my Muslim brothers to do the same. Our community consisted of six of us at the camp. Somehow I was made to be the leader. Yeah, I was the Imam. I didn't run from the responsibility of leading brothers. In fact, I took it as an honor. I felt that Allah was giving me one of my final tests in the Feds before he blessed me with my freedom. I remember some of the older brothers used to tell us in Islamic class that it was very important that we take advantage of knowledgeable brothers while they were around us, because there may come a time when you may have to lead; and so we can know our religion to teach our family.

So on Friday, I would give the Kutba: That's the Religious talk or the "Sermon" at our weekly noonday meeting call Jumah services. During these services I would address the brothers on keeping their faith in Allah and practicing Islam. I would remind them that Allah was in control, not our Ccse manager or any staff members. And if they wanted anything, to pray to Allah, then have patience. These talks weren't just for them. I know I had to lead by example. Practice what I preached, and I did just that. I can remember when my faith paid off.

It was early, 6:30 AM. My regular counselor was on vacation, so a female counselor called my name. She was very nice and I knew it was good news because she was the one that handed out our legal mail. So I knew it was a letter from the courts. The one I had been praying and fasting for. I had to sign for it because it was legal mail. They had to open it in front of me. In my heart, I knew it was the blessing I had been waiting all these years to hear. But I can't lie, I was scared to read it. Over the past 14 years, I had been receiving denials from the courts. And I had so much on the line with this ruling. This could mean my freedom now, or it could keep me in here for the rest of my time, which was 5 more years. All I could think of was, would my mom still be alive and how many more years would I miss seeing my grandson grow up? Then there were thoughts of losing Coretta. She was holding it down for me.

I made it back to my cell. I turned on my night light because it was still dark in the unit. As I opened the letter I was silently praying to myself. Normally I would read the whole letter. This time I skipped straight to the back motion to the last page where the judgement was. There it was in bold letters, GRANTED!! I stared at it like it wasn't real. But it was! The judge ruled in my favor. The first words to come to mind was Allahuh Akbar ("God is great").

My eyes watered up. The tears of joy made their way down my face. After all the years of being rejected with denials from the courts, my time had finally come. I flipped back to the first page. I slowly read the letter from my lawyer. Then I read the motion. It wasn't the immediate release I was expecting. The judge gave me a 4-year reduction on my sentence. That left me with a year to go. But it made me eligible for up to a year in the halfway house. I was still happy for the good news, going to the halfway house was another step forward to being all the way free. I couldn't wait to tell somebody my good news. I didn't care who it was. And it was too early to call my family. So I folded my letter back up and grabbed my work bag and headed out front to the gate where the early morning work crews met up.

I walked with my head held up high like I was Rocky Balboa. The tears were gone, replaced by a big ass smile. The first person to say something was Tank. He hit me with, "What's good, Ahk?"

I didn't answer. I just handed him the letter. That's when Ty jumped in and said, "Oh shit, he done got some time knocked off!"

I shook my head up and down, saying "Yes!"

Tank did the same thing I did when I first opened the letter and went right to the end to see the judgement. He handed it back to me. By then, I had found my voice and told them the whole good news. They all wished me the best and said they were happy a real one got some action! I told them that we were all blessed because we all had dates and we were at the Camp, pointing to the wall in reference to all the brothers that had Life sentences and had already been down for a minute. None of us could deny our blessings when I put it like that. I was flying high with joy. I could hear my mom screaming praise to God once I gave her the news. And my daughter was not going to believe it, she was going to make me tell her over and over again!

My Muslim bro, Tone from Detroit, was the next person I shared my good news with. He worked with me at the gym. Tone was on his way to the halfway house in a few months. He was just as happy as I was to hear I was going home. We worked out every day and had plans to be personal trainers when we got out. Tone was only 32 years old. He looked up to me as an OG. We would spend hours talking about life, business, women, and religion. Today was different. I could taste freedom. The rest of the day went by with me daydreaming of all the things I would soon be doing.

The first thing I did when I got back from working at the gym, was pull out my cell phone. I called my mom first and she responded just like I knew she would. It was a joy to hear her happy, she was holding me down my whole bid. I had to let her know because she had been praying just as hard for this blessing as I was. I called Coretta next. She was happy as well. She went into plan mode. Looking forward to the future of us living together. It was truly a blessing to have Coretta in my corner. I had to wait until my daughter got off work to tell her. But when I did she got to believe it and kept asking me how I found out? And what did they say in the letter? So I just laid the letter out on my bed and took a picture so I could send them to her to read for herself.

I was a real short timer now. Coming to grips with that realization. I knew it was really crunch time. The next day after letting my family know about my time cut. I sat down and wrote down a list of my short term and long term goals. I prioritized my steps on getting back adjusted to the free world. Thinking back on the times I was released from prison focusing on what I knew was mistakes I made. The bigger being not having a real solid plan. In the past, it was all about getting some quick money. Then I would think about what to do with it. This time I would do everything the right way starting with relocating to Atlanta so I could be near my daughter and grandson. I convinced Coretta to move back to Georgia from Texas. The one thing about doing time, that was good. It helped you identify who was really down for you. And after 14 years, my team was small. Going forward my thoughts were on people I would want to help influence my future. I was preparing myself to be around successful people. I needed to build myself a strong support network. I knew opportunities would come my way. And I plan on executing my strategy. The first step was me visualizing myself being successful. Every day I spent time contemplating my moves asking myself questions and then finding answers.

I was waiting for my release date to come. I was executing my plan with every thought that went through my mind. I didn't have that much time left. So I invested the rest of my time and energy on finishing up my first book, Pressure. Then I began writing this book *Federal Pressure*. It was very important to me to complete these books before I got out. In a way they were testing me. To see how serious I was about my plan and could I finish something I set my mind to do. This was my way of earning my freedom from God. Because for one, never in my wildest dreams would I have thought I could write a book on my own. There was the fact that my spelling was terrible. Then what about the self-doubt?

The only way I could ever write a book would be by faith in God. I wanted God to use me, help me share my story. So young guys that read my book could have hope. I had the hard heads, can't get rights, street dudes in mind. Guys that I knew would benefit the most from reading about how God changed my life while dealing with all the pressure we as young black males grew up with. I'm hopeful that every young man that reads my book will see how I overcame my struggles throughout my journey in prison, by writing my story instead of being one of those guys that just sat around allowing the calendar pages to turn.

CHAPTER SEVEN

"I Can't Breathe"

For 8 minutes, 42 seconds (almost 9 minutes!) George begged for his life while four officers held him face down on the ground. But it was the pressure applied by the knee of Derek Chauvin that killed George Floyd in front a crowd of witnesses while they pleaded with the officers to take his knee of MR. Floyd's neck to let him breathe. Thanks to cellphone video, the whole world was able to see how much black lives mean to white police in America. It was heartbreaking to watch, they coldheartedly kill that black brother. And to hear his plea for his life, even calling out to his dead mother. It was chilling to see. The outcry from the public was outraged. Everybody was mad, and hurt, people of all races. After seeing the inconsiderate disregard of human life. This racist whit cop killed George Floyd. If you weren't affected by it in regards to wanting to see change for justice in the way blacks are treated in America, and all over the world. Then chances are you are part of the problem and you are just as racist as the cop that killed George.

The protests that followed were like none I ever seen in my lifetime. Every city in the country came out in protest of police brutality. The chant was "No Justice, No Peace!" and "Enough is Enough!" The people were upset. The outcry was real. The list of names kept growing of dead, unarmed black men and women in the hands of the police. The fact that the officers weren't being charged or convicted was showing the world that black lives didn't matter. A group of black women formed a movement called Black Lives Matter in the wake of Mike Brown being gunned down in Ferguson, Missouri by a white cop. The protest got a boost with the help of Colin Kaepernick, a NFL superstar quarterback, taking a knee during the national anthem. Becoming one of the first biggest celebrities to lose their job for the cause. I remember feeling helpless, sitting in prison without a voice. Every time one of these unjustified killings happened I wanted to be involved somehow. And it wasn't just me, there were other guys in every prison that felt the same way. Whenever a report came over the news, I would look at the expression on the faces of the brothers. And hear the anger in their voices. The tension would be on high. In some of the prisons they would put us on lockdown. Just so no race riots wouldn't jump off. During one of these lock downs after the death of my little homie Trayvon Martin walking to the store for a bag of Skittles. I came up with the idea of Stop B.O.B. Yeah, I know Trayvon wasn't killed by a brother. But my hope was to start a movement of Black Love.

My desire to be a part of the movement would have to wait until I was free. Because it's not easy convincing other people to see your vision. I was coming to the end of my sentence. It was time to create my plan and set goals that help my transition back into society. There were things I could do while I was still in prison like saving my money so I would have something to sustain me for at least the first year. That's the most challenging time for a formerly incarcerated individual the first year out. I needed to create a plan that would lead me to a successful career I could live off. I wanted my books to be my first real product and a service to deliver my message. I intended to share my experience in the streets and prison to help empower anybody that read my story. It doesn't matter whether they were in prison or struggling through life in society, showing them there was always a pathway through pressure. Every step I took towards my freedom, I felt like God was giving me small tests to pass.

During the final year of my imprisonment. At the Camp in ATL. There was a lot of temptation. Majority of the guys there were getting high and drunk. Every night it seemed there was a party. Guys were leaving to meet up with their girl. I have to admit, I badly wanted to leave and meet up with Coretta. The camp was off the chain, but I wasn't. I had no real desire to participate in any of the partying going on all around me. I knew what part of the game I was in, and I was playing to win. No time to waste going backwards. To me smoking weed and drinking was shit I used to do. I've learned that was part of my problem, that led me to prison in the first place. I wanted to prove to God and myself that I didn't need that in my life and I was disciplined enough to be around it without being involved. If I couldn't control myself at the camp. I didn't stand a chance in the real world where the real pressure was. I watched guys come to the camp and change right before my eyes. They started hanging with the party crew. The next thing I knew, they passed out drunk during count time. Most of the time we had good officers working. And they gave them a pass as long as they stayed in their bed and slept it off. There were times when that didn't happen and guys would get locked up and sent back behind the wall. Mess up what little freedom they did have because they couldn't handle their habits. The sad part about this was, most of the guys I'm talking about were older dudes. I'm talking about 40- and 50-year old guys like myself who have been in the system most of their lives. You would think guys so close to going home would have better control of themselves.

This was the time in our sentence, where we were supposed to be building strategies and preparing for reentry to the free world. Not all the guys at the Camp spent their time getting high. There were a few dudes that stayed out the way and focused on getting released on time. In the evening after the 4:00 PM count. I would pull my phone out. Go on line, and see what is happening in the world. Social media was a good source to keep me updated. I started following people that were doing the things that I was into. I was educating myself, studying the moves being made on IG and Facebook. I had to use all the resources I had and my phone was the one for now. The more I learned about social media, the better I could use it to build my brand on IG. I would study people I would want to help influence in my future. I would visualize myself working with these people. I always kept in mind what my good friend Webb had told me about business. It ain't what you know, but who you know, it's all about networking. I also kept myself in good shape because I had a real love for working out.

One of my goals was being a personal trainer, and opening up my own gym. Everybody told me I would make good money training. And that I had the body for it. My whole bid I had trained guys. Now I'm even training a few C.O.s that work at the prison. Everything I had planned to do was centered around the same brand. Deep down in my heart I wanted to be a mentor to at risk young guys. So me opening my own gym, writing books, and personal training were good ways to connect to young guys. I wanted to help them stay out of prison. I had a few names for my brand. The one that personally stood out to me was "V.E.L.I. Life." (Vision, Empower, Leadership, Initiative).

As I wrote in Part 1 of this sequel, Veli is short for Mackaveli, the name of Tupac's 1st CD. It was the name me and my homies pledged our hood on when we all came home from prison. The name our pack had on it and the city respected us by. Back in 96,97 and 98, all the way until they picked up the last of us, Veli was pressure in the streets and jails of Miami. Now I wanted to take what was once a negative part of my life and turn it into a positive statement. I already reached out to Lil Bo aka Bo-aveli, who was now a Muslim. He was still fighting his case in the state joint. He said he would stamp whatever I wanted to do with making Veli a positive brand. Once I'm out, I planned on pulling up on Fred aka Black-aveli. I was hoping he gave me his blessing. I had a backup plan just in case I couldn't get Veil to jump off like I wanted it to.

Life after prison broke down to L.A.P. Season, L.A.P. Fitness, all based around restarting life after getting out of prison. The vision came to me after watching the movement following the death of Nipsey Hussle. Seeing how his brand, The Marathon, had me thinking about life being a long marathon race with everybody running at their own pace. And those of us still locked up not being able to get on the track until we were back in the race of life. Starting over we're way behind everybody else. But with good planning and hard work we should be able to lap a lot of the fakers. The L.A.P. brand was a way for me to express how I felt being left behind. Doing time, people you think care about you will leave you for dead, even some of the same people that you helped in the past. But because you were of no use to them now, they no longer were loyal. With them in mind, that was my motivation for L.A.P. because most of the same people that turned their back on you are the same ones you will see on your way back up. You can call it get back or even selfish, but I don't care.

I want to create a brand that represents the struggle. For those of us that always kept it real, but still got fucked over. From being "trappers" to "lappers", from living life in prison to enjoying life after prison! I had a folder of ideas, real goals, and plans for the future. And as my days drew near for me to go to the halfway house I spent more time getting my mind and spirit prepared. I prayed to God for courage, confidence, with wisdom and understanding on how to reach my goals by serving Him. I accepted the fact that God had a purpose for my life. He was showing me, by giving me another chance at life in the free world. Giving me the opportunity to be the head and not the tail. To lead, not follow.

In my daily talks with my mom, she would often remind me that God had a calling on me. And that I needed to follow my dreams. My mom was very supportive, always encouraging me with her words and with prayers. She was another reason why I had to get it right this time around. I was her only son left and she never gave up on me. My mom was counting on me to take my place as the head of our family. I was determined to make her proud of me, and not let her down. I knew what I had to do and I was ready. At the age of 45, I was on my way to the federal halfway house in Atlanta. After doing 14 and a half years in federal prison, the world had changed so much. And there was a lot I didn't know yet. But I was not worried, I had faith in God. If he brought me to, he will bring me through it. This was the strongest I ever felt in my whole life. And I'm not talking about physical strength. The strength I'm referring to is mental and spiritual. One of the most important lessons I've learned in my prison journey is patience. Learning to live on God's time, trusting in His wisdom to guide me. It's my hope that the reader of this book. Be empowered to never give up. Regardless of where you are in life. If you're in a jail cell facing years in prison or already in prison doing a bid, I want you to know you have power in you to rewrite your story. Remember that God has a purpose for your life and if you are still here alive, then you have the opportunity to sow seeds for a brighter future. I had to learn how to look within myself. And ask them tough questions. The sooner you do that, then the hard work can begin. For me, I started early on in the county jail. Turning to God. I would not have been able to figure out a plan to guide me through decades of prison. Without first figuring out what God's plan for my life. Knowing now that God wanted me to share my story and mentor young guys that felt the same pressure in their lives as I did. The ones like myself, that've been labeled felons, low lifes, and thugs. My message to them is we can overcome those pressures and struggles that we face coming up in the judicial system, prison systems and the hood. I knew with the help of God I will reach the ones he meant for me to help. This was my calling in life. My way of making sense out of years of incarceration.

Nothing can stop a person who chooses to succeed. That's my attitude every day I get up and offer my morning prayer. Then I would sit and reset my mind on what it was I wanted to accomplish for that day. I would not let this time do me. I would make sure to break my time up in three categories: Mental, Spiritual, and Physical. By doing that I felt like I was well balanced in my growth. In all three of these areas, I kept the focus on preparing for my life after prison. Doing time in the Feds taught me to stay ready. And to travel light because you never know when change is going to come. So even though I always planned out my days I always left room for unexpected things like lockdowns and transfers. And as I came to the end of this part of my journey in the federal prison system I spent an hour a day writing my thoughts. This was the part of the book that I wanted to share with the reader …. My return to society.

————————

The process was different from what I ever could have imagined it to be when I first started this bid. We were in a pandemic. Over 150,000 people had died. I couldn't tell you how many from inside the federal system. But I did know from inmate.com that there were a lot of sick inmates behind the wall at Atlanta USP. Right where they told me I was going to quarantine for 22 days before they would release me to go to the halfway house. I was scheduled to leave on 8-26-2020. Quarantine was only supposed to be 14 days before. But for some reason they were sending me early, making me do more days.

When they called my name to go, I was sitting in the TV room eating my lunch. It was 11:00 A.M and I had just got back from working out at the gym. I had an hour to pack. They wanted me and two other guys at the West gate by 12:00 PM. It all was unexpected. Thank God I knew how the Feds operated by now. I was mostly prepared to leave ever since I got the letter from the courts. I've been downsizing my property, giving most of it away. I still hated to rush. I didn't have time to say goodbyes. I was upset about doing the extra days. But I couldn't help but be happy I was finally leaving. All I could do was smile and go with the flow. One step closer to my new life. It was time to put words into action. I was walking by faith, trusting in God to lead me into my purpose and goals in life.

When we walked into the West gate, we were met by an officer who took us to the medical floor. There, we were tested for COVID-19. I didn't want to take the test. My fears were that they were giving us the virus. It wasn't like they haven't done it before. Have you ever heard of the Tuskegee Experiment, where they gave all those brothers gonorrhea? I told myself that if I truly believed in God then there was nothing they could do to me. No matter what I faced or what they put in me, they held no power over my life. I wasn't about to let fear or doubt deny me my freedom. God blessed me with a strong immune system, built with faith in him. Any virus or disease didn't stand a chance. You see, nothing in this world can stop a power that was not from this world. My attitude was "I'm blessed by God." There was a reason why I was going through this process right now. So I humbled myself and waited on that inner voice to kick in.

This time alone put me in a fortunate position. It gave me time to get into deep thoughts. I could concentrate on finishing this book. Also get deeper into my religion, spend more time reading my Quran. I needed this time. They put me in a cell by myself. Lockdown. We only came out on Monday, Wednesday, and Friday for a half an hour. Altogether there were 20 inmates; 10 on the lower deck and 10 on the top deck, where I was. We could use the phone and take showers on our time out. I spent my days reading, working out, and writing. There were guys on the unit that was on their way back behind the fence. They had messed up at the halfway house. So I drilled them for info on the halfway house. I had questions about jobs, home visits, things like that. I was good at listening to other peoples' mistakes, so I learned what not to do.

I was still comprehending my full purpose for having to come through this last experience. Being put back behind the door on lockdown. I knew God was in control and I wasn't being punished. When you're doing God's work everything happens for a reason. It's on you to understand its purpose, we must adjust to how we look at a particular condition we find ourselves in. I always search for the positive in every situation. It didn't take long to come to me.

After I settled down in my cell, my inner voice spoke to. "You need to finish this chapter," it said. "The knee is still on George's neck. Write about the injustice around you."

God wanted me to speak about for the brothers beating on the door at 1:00 AM because his celly had tested positive for Coronavirus. And now he was having shortness of breath. I watched from my cell how the C.O. didn't even want to go near a cell. When they found out there were sick inmates in them. They told us to wear our masks, but never gave us one when we came into the unit. They say it's airborne but we were sharing the same ventilation with the guys that tested positive. All our cells circulate the same air. There wasn't any soap to wash our hands. I was blessed to have my little supplies that I came with from the Camp. There were so many other guys in the unit that were not as fortunate.

I was going to make sure that the world knew the condition my brothers were living under behind these federal walls. "I can't breathe" was still being yelled every day and night from behind cell doors. The pressure of the mighty Federal knee on the necks of helpless inmates. In most cases there was no cell phone video to record the inhumane condition we were living in. Going days without toilet paper, being given cold food to eat for every meal. No fresh water to drink, sleeping on the same linen for weeks. Nothing to clean our cell. I realized God wanted me to feel the pressure again before He released me from it. He gave me a message to deliver with this book. I'm fortunate enough to be leaving this pressure behind me. But God decreed me to carry the message and I've humbled myself to listen to that inner voice in me. By writing Book one *Pressure* and the sequel *Federal Pressure*. I believe God will ignite a flame in whoever he blesses to read the pages of my journey from the hood and throughout the prison system, and back to Him.

Never folding under pressure, keeping the faith, I learned to listen to that voice that's in all of us. I believe in God. Therefore, I will believe in myself. That's the message I want to share with my brothers and sisters still dealing with the pressure of growing up in the hood. For those brothers and sisters that are still dealing with the pressure of being incarcerated, let me share with you a little spiritual encouragement for the Holy Qur'an.

Allah said in the Qur'an, Surah 2:153: "Oh, ye who believe! Seek help with patient perseverance." I can honestly say through my patience and prayers I made it out the belly of the beast aka the Feds. But before I was all the way free, God gave me one last warning. He put me in an environment, similar to the one I began this Federal bid on. Just like the Federal County Jail, my bed was the mat I slept on was just as hard as the metal rack it laid on. It was like the old saying, "You make your bed, you got to lay in it!"

The unit I was in had inmates on all different kinds of time. There were lifers, dudes with long bids, short timers, and even guys that were still on pre-trial. Then there were guys like me waiting to go to the halfway house. I watched a lifer die. He had been 30 years and he was in his 80s. He was sick with the coronavirus for a whole week. We watched while he sat in his cell without eating or drinking anything, nor was he talking to anybody, until one day they came to count us and found him dead. They say the virus killed him, but if you ask me I think he willed himself to death, just tired of doing his time. Losing hope - or never having it all – is the biggest pressure of all.